SEVEN LONGINGS
OF THE
HUMAN HEART

MIKE BICKLE
WITH DEBORAH HIEBERT

FORERUNNER
PUBLISHING
KANSAS CITY, MISSOURI

Seven Longings of the Human Heart
By Mike Bickle with Deborah Hiebert

Published by Forerunner Publishing
International House of Prayer
3535 E. Red Bridge Road
Kansas City, MO 64137

ihopkc.org/books
mikebickle.org

Forerunner Publishing is the book-publishing division of the International
House of Prayer of Kansas City, an evangelical missions organization based
on 24/7 prayer with worship and committed to praying for the release of
the fullness of God's power and purpose, as we actively win the lost, heal
the sick, feed the poor, make disciples, and impact society.

All Scripture quotations, unless otherwise indicated, are from the New
King James Version® of the Bible. Copyright © 1979, 1980, 1982 by
Thomas Nelson, Inc.

Scripture quotations marked (HCSB) are from the Holman Christian
Standard Bible®. Copyright © 2004 by the Holman Bible Publishers.

ISBN: 978-0-9776738-4-1

Cover design by Owen A. Brock, Visual Fluency
Interior design by Dale Jimmo, revised by George Estrada

TABLE OF CONTENTS

The Nature of Longing

There are inescapable cravings in the core of every human heart that cannot be ignored, denied or pacified: they must be *satisfied*. When we wake up in the morning, whether we realize it or not, we are being driven by innate desires that demand answers and refuse delay. These longings are inherent to us as human beings. We have longings, yearnings, placed deep within us by God, for the purpose of wooing us into His grace and presence. As we understand their origin in God, we begin to cooperate with these longings in accordance with His will. We find the answer to our longings in the One who put them within us. His master plan extends even into the realm of our emotions.

Through thirty years of ministry I have been an eager student of human emotions and dynamics. I have enjoyed countless hours listening to people talk about what excites their hearts. What's interesting is that people's longings and needs are not dissimilar and varied; they are common. We have watched thousands of people come through our spiritual community here at the International House of Prayer in Kansas City. Some are internationally-known speakers in their seventies, others are eighteen-year-old interns on their first big adventure away from home. They come from a broad variety of backgrounds, from within the Church and outside of it. Some have large budgets; others have scraped together barely enough support to get by. They come with big moving trucks or with everything they own crammed in a backpack. While no two are exactly the same, I have noticed this interesting commonality among all of them: their *longing*.

Few words in the English language capture such depth of emotion in two short syllables. A longing is not a superficial want that might be satisfied by a simple act of kindness. A longing is not even a genuine need for which we can demand satisfaction. Longing goes deeper than that. A longing is an ache of the heart. It is a cavity of the spirit crying to be filled. In its deepest sense it is neither a true verb nor a true noun, but combines the two, spanning the gap between emotion and genuine need. It is an intangible feeling that ebbs and flows, yet it is a concrete reality. It cannot be reasoned with, negated, or dismissed. If not attended to, it will overtake us. One way or another, whether legitimately or illegitimately, a human longing will be filled. It must be.

As I have observed people and studied the Scriptures, I have identified seven longings that are found in every human heart. These longings are universal and give us insight into the way God designed us. We have cravings built into our spirit as an integral part of our divine design. These cravings reveal the genius of the Creator, who placed these longings in us to reflect His own personality and guide us to—and back to—Him. We are made in His image, and He intentionally planted longings deep within our hearts that only He can fill. He hard-wired us to need, to want, and to find our satisfaction in Him and Him alone. It is the epitome of intelligent design. God's design—both brilliant and diligent—is evidence that He is a jealous God who does not want us to be given over to any lesser pleasure. We were made for *Him*.

The seven longings I have identified are: the longing for the assurance that we are enjoyed by God, the longing to be fascinated, the longing to be beautiful, the longing to be great, the longing for intimacy without shame, the longing to be whole-hearted and passionate, and the longing to make a deep and lasting impact. To understand these longings is to better understand both our struggles and the true purpose of life. They are cravings put into us strategically by God and they entice us into His presence. Though the enemy twists these cravings to tempt us into darkness, they are actually amazing counterparts to characteristics in God's personality and realities in His heart. As with all hunger, these longings have an element of pain, an element of delight, and an element of aching as they woo us into God's presence. When these longings are not fulfilled in God, we are left empty, with pain, mourning, and dissatisfaction. We have built into us a God-shaped vacuum, which remains empty until we allow God to fill it by fulfilling our deepest longings. This gnawing hunger is only sated by God's touch, and never totally fulfilled in this age. Even so, having the merest taste of this satisfaction is to truly live, and having the faintest revelation of that future fulfillment is the pinnacle of what it means to be alive.

This idea of created desire is not entirely foreign to us. When the father of a young child takes him into a swimming pool for the first time, he holds him gently. While never actually giving up control of his son, he allows the child to get a sense of buoyancy, to bob in the water for a moment, in order to demonstrate that this is *not* the playpen. No matter how surefooted the little fellow was on dry land, this is a different environment demanding a different response. If the child is going to survive, he is going to need to hold tightly to his father. From the child's perspective, at first this may all be new and a little scary, but it doesn't take long for him to learn that the answer to his yearning for stability is found in the arms of his father. Dad, in his wisdom, creates the awareness of a need and then presents himself as the obvious answer to the need. His son finds the answer to his longing for safety when he is nearest to his father. The end result is a child who clings closer to his father than he would have had he not been compelled to crave safety.

God is not a haphazard leader or random designer. Everything He does is done with specific intent. In His sovereignty, He put these seven longings in us to help us walk in different facets of privilege as the Bride of Christ. He put these cravings deep within us not so that He could *deprive* us, but so He could *fulfill* us to the uttermost! I often refer to something I call the "superior pleasures of the gospel." God romances our hearts with His Word in such a way as to loosen our grasp from that which is inferior to His kingdom—all the secondary pleasures cluttering our lives—and cause us to be apprehended by the *superior* pleasures of God: those which authentically and eternally satisfy.

Our response to these longings determines our success in life. People spend an inordinate amount of time alternating between denying desires and fulfilling them in unhealthy, ungodly and even destructive ways. Imagine the time and energy we would save if we acknowledged these longings as inescapable, God-given desires, and then positioned our hearts to allow them to be answered and satisfied in the way God intended. The Church must realize that mankind cannot repent for *having* these heart longings, but only for seeking to fulfill them in wrong ways. We cannot repent of the way we were formed by God any more than we can repent of our physical DNA. No one has ever thought of asking God's forgiveness for being tall or having brown eyes. People may or may not like these characteristics, but they don't view them as wrong; they are just a part of who they are. So it is with these longings of the heart. When we learn to embrace them in a healthy, godly way and allow God to answer them— with the only true satisfaction—then we will begin to touch the superior pleasures of the gospel and enter into the joyous realm of living for which we were created.

CREATED FOR PLEASURE

While the Puritans contributed greatly to the spiritual DNA of our country, one of their unfortunate legacies is the tendency some had of viewing all pleasure as evil. These attitudes have stayed with American Christians for generations—if something is enjoyable, it is viewed with suspicion and disdain. How could something be godly and enjoyable at the same time? One of our staff members remembers his Bible college professor explaining how he was raised believing that anything pleasurable was sinful. During his childhood he was never allowed to play any sport that involved a ball. "Daddy wouldn't let us play basketball or baseball," the professor explained. "We'd always ask him how he knew those things were a sin, and he'd tell us, 'If it's round, it's wrong!'"

Of course, we'd like to think we've outgrown these kinds of attitudes, and indeed most of the Church has loosened its legalistic grip on things; but we have retained the core belief that things that give us pleasure, even emotional pleasure, are somehow wrong and must be rejected. The result is a Church full of people with genuine God-given longings who lecture one another on why it's wrong to feel the way they do. Meanwhile, God is crying out to them, "I made you that way!"

We can't repent our way out of these longings, but we can only satisfy them within the context of the gospel. If we are going to walk in the kind of resiliency and victory needed to face the ever-increasing onslaught of demonic deception and rage, these seven longings must be answered. Our temptation is to try to satisfy these longings in unsanctified ways. Of course, Satan is more than willing to accommodate us in this endeavor. Pulled by our sinful nature, we too often succumb to the lure of satisfying these longings in wrong ways. Fulfilling them in a right way will make us victorious in our hearts and enable us to resist pride, covetousness, pornography, the occult, bitterness, rage and the like. We are not to live without power and without hope.

Because Satan is master of the counterfeit, each longing finds a counterfeit fulfillment in our fallen nature. The young woman, looking to satisfy her God-given capacity to feel love, gives her heart and body to a young man who is struggling in exactly the same way. Both of them find temporary answers to eternal longings, but when the gloss wears off, they're simply lonely together. Many a marriage has begun in such a manner, only to dissolve later when mere physical attraction cannot withstand the pressures of children, a mortgage, or a lack of common interests. In another example, the busy executive, fully aware of his capacity for greatness, misinterprets greatness to mean worldly acclaim. Twenty years later he finds himself at the top of his career. Houses, cars, and travel are at his disposal. In a moment of brutal honesty, he admits that it all leaves him empty. He reached for the brass ring and found it attached to nothing.

Our newspapers and neighborhoods are full of stories just like this. Since Cain killed Abel, people have had one wrong idea after another as to how they could fulfill the longing to make a difference. In the end they find themselves disappointed, empty-hearted, and hating the very longings that got them there. Consider for a moment how God must feel about this; He created these priceless longings only to watch men and women pursue a false fulfillment. How He longs for His people to position their hearts and their hunger rightly, and in doing so, to encounter the surprise of their lives—the pleasures of God which satisfy beyond measure.

ETERNAL LONGING

Not only are our longings universal, they are eternal. They are not limited to our relationship with God in this age. God did not intend for our longings to go away after this life. In fact, they and their fulfillment will be even greater in the age to come. In this age there will be moments when we experience great things in God. These satisfactions are God's beautiful gift to sustain our hearts. Much of life can seem devoid of the experience of God's touch, and even a little movement of His Spirit toward ours results in moments of great satisfaction. Even though these experiences are God-given and impacting, they are still temporary and need to be repeated. Periodic touches from God give us strength to continue on in our race. The remembrance of them keeps us reaching to experience them yet again. All of this works together in God's divine plan. He touches tender and vulnerable areas of our hearts and these divine touches stay with us for a season. We long, His presence comes, and when it lifts we are left more in love, with more longing for Him than we had before. The Creator places longings within us which can only be answered by and in Him. He then answers the longings in part, giving us just enough satisfaction to sustain us in the pursuit, and leaving just enough of an ache to keep us on the journey. The nature of being wooed demands an ebb and flow of desire and satisfaction. A billion years from now, we will still long for these things. They will play a key part in the way we will be fascinated by God for eternity.

Why did God place these longings within us? Surely He knew we would run to and fro, finding temporary relief in counterfeit answers. Getting an understanding of the nature of these seven longings and God's desire to be their sole fulfillment helps us understand both our struggle and our purpose in life in a whole new way. The longings are dynamically connected to who God is, and no amount of makeshift or false pleasures can compare with their ultimate fulfillment. Each longing is a means by which we can understand God more deeply, just as it is an essential part of His beauty in our lives. The pleasures we gain when we allow God to fulfill our longings are eternal—they will last forever and ever.

THE BRIDAL PARADIGM

One of the greatest foundational truths about God and His people is that Jesus Himself is the eternal Bridegroom and we, as the Bride of Christ, are the ones chosen by God to be His eternal partner. Understanding this gives us insight into how we were formed and our reason for existence. Before the creation of the world, the Father wanted His Son to have a bride. All of history—from the fall of man to the cross of Christ and every instance of repeated sin and offered redemption—builds toward the great climactic event called the marriage supper of the Lamb (Revelation 19:7-8).

Jesus' death on the cross served a dual purpose. It provided redemption for humanity while simultaneously providing a way for the Son to have a worthy Bride, a partner equal in every way. We are familiar with the cross and how it buys us redemption, but we don't always consider the fullness of why we were redeemed. Why has God closed so wide a gap and walked out so baffling a mission? It was for the purpose of bringing mankind, the redeemed saved by grace, into the embrace of a Bridegroom King. We will never understand our longings—desires crying out night and day and refusing to be silenced—unless we first understand this truth about God as a passionate Bridegroom and begin to relate to Him from the standpoint of a cherished bride. I often describe this perspective on life, this interpretation of who we are to God and who He is to us, as the "bridal paradigm." It is a paradigm or perspective of a God who enjoys us and is filled with affection for us, embracing us even in the midst of our weakness and stumbling.

A paradigm is an example that serves as a pattern or model for thought. We are not always aware of the paradigms with which we view life; however, our paradigms color every experience we have. What we think, how we speak, how we interpret the past and how we anticipate the future—all these things are affected by our paradigms. A visitor to Washington, DC, for example, looks at the United States Capitol with a very different paradigm than a powerful senator. Both have a right to be there, but one walks with much more confidence than the other. The senator understands that he is expected to be there. Within the briefing rooms and the Senate chamber he commands a measure of respect. Likewise, he knows who the senior members of the Senate are and when to defer to them. The senator operates with an authority paradigm. The tourist who just stepped off the train, unfamiliar with the security precautions and many protocols of the Senate, walks tentatively. He is welcome in the Capitol, but the business of the country does not hinge on his contribution. Interestingly enough, the tourist notices things the senator has long ignored, like the ornately-carved ceilings or vast tile floors. He operates with a visitor's paradigm. The tourist and the senator will walk the same hallways, see the same sights, and meet many of the same people, but will have very different experiences because of their very different paradigms.

The bridal paradigm describes a specific perspective of the kingdom of God. While it is not a term found in Scripture, it is a helpful phrase that conveys this distinct paradigm of God, and so is essential to our spiritual journeys and pursuit of Him. This focus draws together specific biblical themes relating to the beauty of Jesus as the heavenly Bridegroom and the impartation of His beauty to His eternal Bride, the Church. The bridal paradigm changes the way we understand and absorb many scriptures, because it honors the larger body of truth in the Bible. It enables us to rejoice in the whole of Scripture. Written over thousands of years, by forty different authors (most of whom did not know one another), it is astounding how the Bible shows such unity in theme and purpose. Out of the vastness of Scripture, the Holy Spirit will often draw us into a particular focus for a season. Such a focus functions as a smaller current within the great river of the gospel of Christ.

The bridal paradigm of the kingdom of God is one such focus that has a glorious impact on our hearts (though, of course, the whole of Scripture is necessary). I have found it helpful to name this focus in order to more clearly identify the power of its elements. The real strength of this paradigm is seen in its unique combination of the truths captured in the whole package. The more you study, the more you will find hints of the bridal paradigm throughout the Word of God.

When you search the Scriptures, you find many different pictures of the kingdom of God. The kingdom of God is likened to the fishing industry, as we are told to be fishers of men. Those who are evangelists live with a fishing paradigm. Wherever they go, they see people who need Jesus and "cast a net." The metaphors of sowing, pruning, reaping, and grafting lend themselves well to the kingdom's likeness to agriculture. West of Kansas City, the Great Plains area spreads a thousand miles, north to south. To the families who farm those fields, the agricultural paradigm is very real. They understand well the nature and process of reaping and planting. The kingdom is often referred to in a war paradigm, with Scripture passages about fighting, sacrifice, suffering, and government. Any soldier can quickly offer you countless examples of how authority relates to the kingdom of God.

All of these paradigms are genuine and worthy of study, but as we near the return of Jesus, I believe the spiritual paradigm God is emphasizing with the greatest urgency is the bridal paradigm. I often speak of the generation in which Jesus returns as the "Bridegroom generation," because in that generation many believers will interpret the kingdom of God in this light. This view of God and of ourselves will equip our hearts with holy affection to endure the greatest trouble in all of human history, and will prepare us to stand in pure love and bright righteousness at Jesus' return.

In His last public sermon before His crucifixion, Jesus declared, "The kingdom of heaven is like a certain king who arranged a marriage for his son" (Matthew 22:2). Knowing what has now been revealed to us, we can imagine the gleam in Jesus' eye, understanding that His Father was the "certain King" who was planning His own wedding. Scripture makes it clear that God possesses a hidden plan in His heart that will culminate in a wedding celebration at the end of natural history (Revelation 19:7-8). By the indescribable grace of God, this human Bride, the promised inheritance, cleansed and freed from sin, will be enthroned, embraced, and adorned by Jesus Himself as she rules with Him (Revelation 3:21). This is the purpose for which we were created. From Genesis 1 on, the Bible makes this clear. Out of the burning heart of Jesus comes forth a river of longing for His people that will be satisfied in the fullness of history—and it is *our* story!

I firmly believe that the bridal paradigm of the kingdom, given by Christ in His final earthly message, is the most powerful method used to transform the human heart. It is the last paradigm Jesus emphasized at His first coming, and it will be the final one the Holy Spirit emphasizes to the Church worldwide before Jesus' second coming. I realize that this is a bold statement, but I believe it is a scriptural one.

> And the Spirit and the bride say, "Come!" (Revelation 22:17)

This passage records a cry that will arise from both the Holy Spirit and the Bride of Christ. They will join voices in one clarion call to Jesus. The Messiah will return to be enthroned on earth as God's human King—fully God, fully man. But what ushers this in? The joint call of the Spirit and the Bride. Although there will be unprecedented spiritual warfare at the end of the age, Scripture does not say, "The Spirit and the army." Although we will function as a spiritual family, it is not "the Spirit and the family" crying out for Jesus to return. At the end of the age, He's coming back in response to the Spirit-led cry of the Church in her primary identity as the Bride.

People obey God for a variety of reasons. Many are motivated out of a fear of punishment. Like whipped dogs, they cower in the corner and watch for the twitch of the master's hand. In their minds, God spends most of His time angry, and, if they misstep, the fury of heaven will be unleashed upon them. Ironically, these people often serve as the volunteer base of the local church. They may be serving in the wrong area of ministry, but they stepped in to fill a hole out of fear that God would punish them if they didn't. Misery becomes a part of their identity in Christ. These people often make the right decisions for holiness, but are empty, and sometimes even angry, while doing so. Unbelievers watch them and think, "Surely this is the worst of both worlds." Other believers are motivated out of a sense of superiority. Their obedience displays that they have in fact heard the voice of God and responded. In their minds, it's important to be known among the brethren as ones who are radically obedient, because it makes them feel better than the rest. Like those motivated by fear, these people also often make right decisions. Unfortunately, they receive the majority of their reward before men in this age (Matthew 6:1-18). At the end of their days, they will have lived long, obedient lives that have been primarily motivated by the fear of man.

Affection-based obedience is an entirely different thing. Affections are unique to human beings; there is nothing in the Scripture about angels having affections. They have joy and other emotions, but these are not affections. Only human beings have been given the dignity of possessing burning desire and affectionate love. God gave us this nobility so we might voluntarily choose Him in love with all of our hearts, souls, minds, and strength. A life characterized by affection-based obedience is a life in which a person knows that he or she is so loved by God, and so loves God in return, that obedience is the only reasonable response to anything God wishes. For the sake of love, they give everything and find no sacrifice too great. This is what God intends for all of us. As we view ourselves and position our hearts in the spiritual identity of voluntary lovers, rather than timid or manipulated workers, something powerful begins to be awakened. This truly is who we are. And this is the bridal paradigm. God uses this mindset, this bridal paradigm, to motivate us to affection-based obedience and lovesick holiness.

Before the return of the Lord, the Church will have a fierce and determined spirituality based on affection for God. Passion for Jesus accompanied by extravagant obedience will be the norm among believers around the world. Two great trends will occur in the Church at the same time. One, the great falling away of the Church, will be countered by the other, the great ingathering of souls and maturing of the Church (2 Thessalonians 2:3; Revelation 7:9-14). Paul described a Church worldwide that will be spotless and blameless in character (Ephesians 5:26–32). This character will be both the product of the Holy Spirit's work and the by-product of the unprecedented circumstances called the Great Tribulation (Matthew 24:21). The bridal paradigm will be the most effective way to live in that time; this passionate view of God will empower us to stand fearlessly in our obedience.

WHY LIVE BY THE BRIDAL PARADIGM?

Some may ask, "Why is the bridal paradigm necessary? I've gotten along fine in this life without thinking of God in this way. Why is it imperative to start now?" There are many answers to this question, but I'll give you just a few. The bridal paradigm offers a framework to live an energized life in Christ, relating to Him as more than just a healer who heals and a savior who forgives. Yes, He is forever our healer and savior, but He is also a lover, a God who is lovesick for us. We pray differently to God when we know that His primary motivation is desire for us and that His passion is to have our attention—indeed, we find ourselves growing more deeply in love for Him. Since the days of Mary and Martha (Luke 10:38–42), we have been aware that the kingdom of God is populated by both workers and lovers. We all fall somewhere along that spectrum and, if we are honest with ourselves, would admit to moving back and forth between the two from time to time. Over the years, I have noticed something: lovers will outwork workers *every* time.

Thirty-three years ago, under the lights of a high school football game, my brother suffered a horrific collision that resulted in a broken neck. Of course, he was immediately rushed to the hospital, but the damage was already done. He is totally paralyzed to this day. I have been in and out of hospitals with him over the last thirty-three years. In the early years we spent months at a time in rehabilitation hospitals. Once in a while we would see a nurse fall in love with a patient. It didn't happen often, but every now and then a worker would change their relationship with the patient to become a lover. It was interesting to see how when a worker became a lover, they could throw their nursing checklist out the window and serve out of love, not needing a list to remind them of what their beloved needed. The endurance and energy demonstrated by a nurse who had fallen in love with a patient was astounding. They would work much harder because of love than they ever did when it was just their job. My point is that love is a much more powerful motivator than duty. Love changes the way we respond to the will of another. Being a lover of God will transform how we live for Him, and having the bridal paradigm, in which we understand that Jesus is our Bridegroom and we are His Bride, is essential if we are to think of Him as an eternal lover.

The generation in which the Lord returns will be characterized by a level of emotional brokenness unprecedented in human history. The perversion and woundedness of the human heart will reach previously unimagined proportions. Sinful perversion, occult activity, divine judgment and widespread martyrdom will reach levels of intensity mankind has never known. The pornography industry and the occult will both continue to intersect with rapidly-growing technology. Jesus described the last generation as being filled with bitterness, offense, and betrayal, with people's hearts growing cold (Matthew 24:10–14). In that dark and pressing time, the Church will need to see herself as a Bride who has a jealous Husband on His way to deliver her. God has strategically reserved the fullest expression of the bridal paradigm for the unique and complex pressures of the last generation. It is God-inspired to empower the Church to overcome the coldest, most lawless, fearful, demonic, and sexually perverted generation in history.

Jesus is going to cleanse His Church, washing us with the Word, and present us to Himself as something more glorious than we can imagine. He absolutely *will* bring His people to victory, to a place of power, of lovesickness, and of triumph over sin. Paul wrote, "that He [Jesus] might sanctify and cleanse her [the Church] with the washing of water by the word, that He might present her to Himself a glorious church, not having spot or wrinkle or any such thing, but that she should be holy and without blemish" (Ephesians 5:26-27). This reference to having no spot or wrinkle is not merely speaking of our legal standing of justification—obviously we will stand blameless, because Jesus died for us. It also refers to the actual building of character in the people of God as we come into full cooperation with Him. Jesus will accomplish it without violating anyone's free will.

There is nothing more powerful or pleasurable than when God reveals God to the human spirit. This washing and presentation to Christ can only be accomplished as the Church steps into her identity as the Bride of Christ, who loves Jesus just as the Father loves Him (John 17:26). Paul did not say that Jesus would wash a family or an army or a farmer. He said Jesus would purify and cleanse His *Bride*.

The Church will be empowered by the grace of God until she overflows with holy lovesickness for her Bridegroom Messiah. *It takes God to love God.* We need the Spirit's impartation of God's love to equip us to love God. *Our desire for God is God's gift to us.* Our love and desire for God is an expression of His desire for us. All the emotional resources necessary for God's people to walk victoriously in love will flow out of our enjoyment of God as we walk in our bridal identity.

As we consider these seven longings of the human heart, begin to look at them as a road map to viewing the Lord as our Bridegroom and ourselves as His chosen eternal companion. There is a delightful redundancy, in that in order to fulfill these longings we must see Jesus as our Bridegroom, and in order to see Him as a Bridegroom, we must come to Him to satisfy our longings. We will never be satisfied in the pursuit of false and temporary fulfillments. Only when we begin to touch and experience some of these eternal satisfactions will we be empowered to let go of the inferior ones. No matter how easy it is to prop up our lives with counterfeit pleasures, we must give ourselves in wholehearted pursuit of the pleasures that will carry us now, and continue to carry us even billions of years from now.

Sin is pleasurable, and sin appears to be the most pleasurable thing the human spirit can experience. Satan did not invent pleasure, he perverted it and offered empty substitutes that can never satisfy. The difference between false pleasures and the truth of the romance of the gospel, of God revealing Himself to the human spirit, is as different as the counterfeit always is from the purity of the real thing. The superior pleasures of the Spirit are far more powerful than the inferior pleasures of sin, and supernatural emotional strength and power will be vital in light of the coming global crisis of social, spiritual, economic, political, and emotional disruption. Only satisfied people who are happy in God will be equipped to stand in that hour. Thus, the seven longings related to the bridal paradigm are significant for today. Paul prayed that we would be strengthened with divine might in the inner man (Ephesians 3:16). God will do this as He releases truth into our hearts.

The realm of pleasure belongs squarely in God's camp. While God has certainly granted us physical pleasures, emotional pleasures, and mental pleasures, the most profound pleasures are spiritual in nature. This is evident when the Holy Spirit reveals the Son to the human spirit. The superior pleasures of the gospel are implied in Matthew 22:2. When Jesus referred to the kingdom as a bridegroom and bride at a wedding, He was pointing to a whole new arena of experience in redemption— the experience of being an eternally-cherished bride. Tragically, the inferior pleasures of sin have the potential to dominate our lives if they are the only pleasures we experience. If someone has not experienced God, or has very little knowledge of who He is, the inferior pleasure of sin seems a worthy fulfillment, rather than the hollow counterfeit we know it to be.

Many Christians focus only on resisting the inferior pleasures Satan offers. They look at their sin and promise God, "I'll never, ever, *ever* do that again!" They make promises they can't keep and go through religious incantations as they seek to be set free. Still, in the back of their minds they're remembering that their sin was pleasurable—it was wrong, but it still felt good. It was sin, but it was the only pleasure they'd ever known. They struggle to live their lives in Christ, but if they were honest, they'd admit that they consider their days before coming to Jesus as "the good old days."

God's desire is to awe us with the pleasures available only in relationship with Him. He taps us on the shoulder and whispers, "Turn around! Look at the superior pleasures, the beauty of My Son, the greatness of who you are in God—My chosen partner who will rule and reign with Me forever and ever!" It is when we fix our eyes on these things, on the greater pleasures of God, that something happens in our hearts. The first commandment shifts into first place and we begin to live for Him wholeheartedly. The pleasures sin had to offer suddenly appear as they really are: cold, hollow, and always demanding our time, attention, and energy, while butchering our hearts piece by piece. Covetousness, pornography, and bitterness are not nearly as powerful when we're brushing up against the superior pleasures of God and touching the vast enjoyment within His person. When the scales are removed from our eyes, we realize just how much God has to offer, and that what He has to offer is precisely what we've been chasing after.

The master plan of God is an amazing thing. He created a Bride for His Son, watched her fall into imperfection, and then offered His Son to redeem the Bride for Himself. All along God rested, confident in knowing He had endowed the Bride with longings that she could not ignore. He knew the enemy would use those longings to manipulate Jesus' Bride. Even this did not make God nervous. He knew what He had to offer. As she has run from place to place trying to fulfill her longings, God has remained confident that she would only find fulfillment in returning to the identity and destiny for which she was created—to be the Bride of Christ. She will have to come home to a holy romance if she is ever to be truly happy.

To be clear, when I refer to holy romance, I'm not referring to anything related to Jesus and sexuality. The concept of a holy romance is a truth contained in the Word of God: being delighted by God's beauty, feeling the spiritual pleasures of the Word, feeling the Spirit resonating inside, and understanding what it means to be loved by God. It's also called "the fullness of joy" (Psalm 16:11). Fullness of joy is a massive reality. It's more than just feeling good about a circumstance and claiming a sense of victory, it's a genuine way of life. Paul the apostle spoke brilliantly of this romance when he said, "For I reckon that the sufferings of this present time are not worthy to be compared with the glory which shall be revealed in us" (Romans 8:18). There was no exaggeration in that statement.

Paul was a man romanced by the gospel. His heart was exhilarated. He was a lovesick man. In Philippians 3:8, he spoke about counting the cost. He was in essence saying, "Everything that I gave up, my entire career, all the family lineage I had going for me—it is rubbish, it means nothing to me. Do not talk about me giving up stuff because it only tells me that you do not understand how to live. I did not give up anything, I brought nothing to the table, in light of what is truth." Why did he say this? Because the reward of a lover is the power to love, and that's exactly what he had. He was able to truly receive God's love for him and in so receiving was empowered to love God in return. A lover's reward is love reciprocated. We know it is the desire of God to unlock the hearts of His people; He is going to bring us into the superior pleasures of the gospel. He is going to cause us to know obedience rooted in lovesickness. My premise is that the bridal paradigm is the most powerful gospel truth in terms of transforming the human heart and empowering it to love. The bridal paradigm has the most powerful impact on our emotional chemistry.

Friends, the Great Commission will not be fulfilled without martyrs. Many ministries in the coming hour, even in the Western church, will be sufficiently anointed to equip "joyful martyrs." There are more believers being martyred worldwide in this time than at any other time in history. Until now the Western church has been largely exempt from this suffering. That will soon change. The apostle John had a vision that revealed the prominent role that martyrs will play in the last days.

> When He opened the fifth seal, I saw under the altar the souls of those who had been slain for the word of God and for the testimony which they held. And they cried with a loud voice, saying, "How long, O Lord, holy and true, until You judge and avenge our blood on those who dwell on the earth?" Then a white robe was given to each of them; and it was

> said to them that they should rest a little while lon-
> ger, until both the number of their fellow servants
> and their brethren, who would be killed as they
> were, was completed. (Revelation 6:9-11)

What will empower these martyrs? They will experience a deep spiritual intimacy with Jesus. This intimacy will be the result of feasting on the knowledge of the beauty and majesty of Jesus, the Bridegroom King. These martyrs will abundantly experience the superior pleasures of the gospel in accordance with the bridal paradigm of the kingdom. John described a victorious multitude of joyful, worshiping martyrs at the end of the age.

> And I saw…those who have the victory over the
> beast…standing on the sea of glass, having harps of
> God. (Revelation 15:2)

The book of Revelation encourages the Church to come home to her Husband. It affirms the legitimacy of the longings that the Bride has so long denied, and assures us that those longings are not at odds with how God created us.

As we explore these seven longings, imagine with me for a moment what it would be like to finally find the utter fulfillment of your deepest, most inescapable desires. Begin to imagine what it would be like to have these longings totally satisfied—if you woke up one day and found yourself completely whole and fully functioning in pure, unadulterated delight. If the burning longings that have haunted you for as long as you've been aware of them were fulfilled, if suddenly all your needs were met, *who would you be?* I'm trusting you'll find out that you would be who you were created to be, a person rooted and grounded in the incomprehensible love of Christ, filled with holy passion for God, and deeply satisfied by His ardent passion for you.

CHAPTER ONE

The Longing to Be Enjoyed by God

The Lord jealously desires that we believe that He sincerely enjoys us in a personal way. We were created for this. There is no way to avoid our deep need for this. He orders our seasons and days around this distinct objective.

In my own personal journey, there is one day I will never forget, a day that formed this truth in my heart so specifically and tangibly that it marked me forever. I had spent the day in my lonely apartment, seeking the Lord in prayer, reaching for Him in the study of His Word and pursuing Him in every way I knew how. Hours went by with little or no evidence of any sort of breakthrough. As the day grew longer, my heart grew heavier with feelings of loneliness and the uncertainty of why I was spending my time and my strength in such a way.

After long hours of what seemed to be futile disciplines, I spread open my arms with one last request for God. I simply said, "Enjoy me." It was then that I was flooded with the piercing truth that God did enjoy me, and I was instantly set free from the cloud of accusation, rejection, and shame under which I had found myself. I had nothing to offer, except a heart that said yes to Him, however weak and feeble it was. That day, God convinced me that it was not about me or anything I could do, but only about a God who enjoys me and has unyielding affection for me.

—Deborah Hiebert

THE NEED TO BE ENJOYED

It has been said that you see what people are made of when they struggle. While it's true that pressure displays a person's character, there's something equally revealing about success. Sally Field's speech when she won her second Oscar in 1985 is an example. Having ascended to the podium to receive the Oscar, Field revealed a common longing of the human heart—to be enjoyed. Speaking candidly, she admitted to the crowded theater, "I haven't had an orthodox career, and I've wanted more than anything to have your respect. The first time [I won] I didn't feel it, but this time I feel it, and I can't deny the fact that *you like me right now, you like me!*"

That six-second speech pointed to the most fundamental of the seven longings of the human heart: the longing for the assurance that we are enjoyed. While we most naturally look for fulfillment of this in receiving affirmation from others, our true longing to be enjoyed is rooted in our desire to be enjoyed by God Himself. We were created by a God who enjoys loving us, and He designed us to need this assurance from Him. When we understand the truth of God's enjoyment, our hearts become strong and bold in response.

The fulfillment of this longing begins only as we truly understand the finished work of the Cross. God certainly forgives us, but He also enjoys us. He truly desires our fellowship. This is remarkable. After we first understand *what* Jesus did on the Cross, then we seek to understand *why* He did it. He desires and delights in us for reasons bigger than anything we can secure by our dedication or achievements.

The extravagant emotions God feels for us fulfill our longing to be enjoyed and are expressed in two distinct ways: as a Father and as a Bridegroom. The Father has affection for us as His children, and Jesus has passion for us as His Bride. This understanding gives us the foundation to identify with and enter into what I call the "romance of the gospel." We feel enjoyed by God and exhilarated in God's love and joy.

The Song of Solomon is an eight-chapter love song. It is first a natural love song that extols the glory and beauty of married love. It is powerful at the natural level, but it has a spiritual interpretation as well. We do not have to choose one over the other; both of them are powerful and necessary. In the spiritual, or allegorical interpretation, on two occasions the Bride, the Church, stands before Jesus, the Bridegroom, and cries out, "I am lovesick!" (Song of Solomon 2:5; 5:8). She then goes on to proclaim the truth that God's very *desire* is towards her (Song of Solomon 7:10).

Our lives have value and importance specifically because God enjoys us. This may all seem too good to be true, but it is true—gloriously true. We are defined by the One who pursues us. We are not just the sum total of what we accomplish. We are defined as important by virtue of the One who wants us, loves us, and enjoys us. Our success is measured solely by the fact that Jesus values and desires us. Our ministry may never be large, we may never have a lot of money, or even a lot of friends, but the fact that He enjoys us answers the greatest need of our hearts. When we comprehend and accept this truth, our hearts are set on fire.

THE POWER OF FEELING ENJOYED

After failing in sin, some people cast themselves into "spiritual probation." God does not impose this on them; they bring it on themselves. They take a week or a month or two to beat themselves up to prove how sorry they are—as a sort of penance. When we fail and then sincerely repent before Jesus, we can be assured that we continue as first-class citizens in His kingdom. There is no need to relegate ourselves to some sort of probationary period before returning to the Lord. He would rather we just repent and push delete on the whole mess, and then run back into His presence crying, "Here I am, Lord! Your beloved! Here I am!" We need to get right back up without slowing down in our pursuit of Him. When our hearts are assured that we can be fully known by God and still enjoyed by Him, something powerful happens in our emotional chemistry. We discover a confidence in God never before imagined. This is startling news: God enjoys sincere believers, even in their immaturity!

Our culture does not understand a God who enjoys people. God has been portrayed in a variety of ways, but usually as a grumpy old man who looks down stiffly on fun-loving humans. While the Bible gives us an accurate picture of God as righteous Judge of the earth, most people have misinterpreted this and pictured God as being the God of punishment. They've concentrated on the judgment while ignoring the righteousness that demands it. Many believers are not entirely sure that God ever even thinks of them, and figure that if He does, He's probably disappointed, if not downright angry. Nothing could be further from the truth. What we must lay hold of is that God rejoices over us just like a bridegroom rejoices over his bride.

> As a bridegroom rejoices over [his] bride, so your
> God will rejoice over you. (Isaiah 62:5)

Much of our misunderstanding of God's character springs from our personal histories. At some point in their life journey, almost everyone has opened their heart to another person, only to find such vulnerability met with apathy, rejection, or even scorn. Perhaps you were the first-grader who fully understood that the teacher was less than fair with the treats. You may have been the fifteen-year-old boy who mustered the courage to pass a note to the girl sitting near you in study hall, only to see the note shredded, along with your heart. More poignantly, you may have been the adult who, in a moment of candor, whispered, "I love you," and waited in awkward silence while the object of your affection withheld the same affirmation. The fear of rejection is learned behavior, and our earthly relationships offer us plenty of opportunity to learn it.

Nothing is as tender or raw as a bruised lover. The portion of our hearts that longs for love may become calloused on the surface as we vow, "I won't let that happen again." But just below the surface sits a mass of bruised tissue, reminding us every day, "It hurts to be unloved and unwanted." The irony of it all is that we are desired by God. While we preoccupy ourselves with trying to fulfill our longing with the affirmation of others, God waits to reveal His affection to us.

> *As a young child, I experienced significant rejection by my peers. I was on my way to believing that God rejected me just like they did. When God broke in with this understanding of His enjoyment over me, somehow, in my childlike heart, I actually experienced and felt that God liked me. At recess I would find myself all alone, singing songs to the One who enjoyed hearing my voice. Something powerful took place in my emotions as I received the first seeds of the amazing discovery that God delighted in me. —Deborah Hiebert*

VALUE COMES FROM DESIRABILITY

The misunderstandings many people have about God have led to confusion about what it means to be a person of value. We assume that our ultimate value is derived from our contributions. When we contribute to a group or individual, we expect them to value us. While we may gain recognition from our peers, the value is usually placed on our work rather than on our person. The Oscar was awarded to Sally Field for what she did, not for who she was. Our value is not determined by our actions, but by Who it is that desires us. What makes a house increase in value? The simple fact that someone wants it. One of our International House of Prayer leaders grew up in rural North Dakota, where you can buy a house for a fraction of what it would cost in a major city—same floor plan, same construction materials, same amount of time to build it. So what is the difference? The location of a house in a major city makes it desirable for a greater number of people. Is the house better suited for use? No, but it is more valuable because value is derived from desirability. By that simple standard, you have great value because you are desired by God. He enjoys you beyond measure.

The gospel of Luke dedicates chapter 15 to stories about how much God values, is exhilarated by, and enjoys human beings. As Jesus spoke to a crowd of Pharisees, He illustrated what religious people have struggled to understand for centuries—that God enjoys His people and will go to great lengths to pursue them. He searches for us like a woman searches for a lost coin, or a good shepherd seeks out one lost sheep. Jesus emphasized how God rejoices when prodigals return to Him.

> "What man of you, having a hundred sheep, if he loses one of them does not...go after the one which is lost until he finds it? And when he has found it, he lays it on his shoulders, rejoicing." (Luke 15:4-5)

> "Or what woman, having ten silver coins, if she loses one coin, does not...search carefully until she finds it...saying, 'Rejoice with me, for I have found the piece which I lost!' Likewise, I say to you, there is joy in the presence of the angels of God over one sinner who repents." (Luke 15:8-10)

The passage ends with the story of a wealthy man who had two sons. One of the sons was the boy every parent hopes for. He was faithful, obedient, and attentive to his father. The other son was what we commonly call a "problem child." He was demanding and insolent and rejected his family, insisting on an early inheritance and the freedom to roam. Eventually, the wild child found himself, like so many others in rebellion, at the end of his rope. He was knee-deep in the mire, a lost Jewish boy sharing a plate with a pig. Being of a people who would not eat pork, the message was clear—he had become what everyone in his culture despised.

God is gracious in that He often grants a moment of clear-headedness even in the midst of a season of sin. As the boy knelt for dinner at the pig trough, he had one of those moments: "My father's servants have it better than this. I may not be able to return as a son, but surely I can return as a slave." In coming to a place of regret, he arrived at the same place many of us do. What he did next, however, is what separates those who find grace from those who do not. He turned his heart toward home. Rather than remain in his misery, he chose to take a risk and act upon his regret. A great *what if* arose in his spirit: *What if I took a chance? What if I approached my Father? What might He do?*

Most likely, he had a best-case scenario in his head that went something like this: *Dad will allow me to live in the barn and work in the fields. It'll be safe. It'll never be comfortable, but it'll be safe. There'll be no pigs.* That's the same thing most people think when considering a return to God: *I'll escape the worst of hell, but will never have the best from God's heart.* They couldn't be more wrong.

If you've ever had a child get lost in a store, you know that you look everywhere for them. I've heard stories of parents whose children were abducted. For years they look in stores, on the street, on school buses, always hoping for the unlikely, always hoping their child will be returned. That's precisely what this father was doing.

> "When [the prodigal] was still a great way off, his father saw him and had compassion, and he ran and fell on his neck and kissed him." (Luke 15:20)

Jesus told this story for one reason: He wanted to give us a picture of how much God enjoys us. He enjoys us so much that when we start taking those first shaky steps in His direction, or back in His direction, He runs out to meet us with overwhelming affection. Many people approach God tentatively, aching for a connection with Him but secretly expecting a thrashing once they get close. They imagine that it is safer to run *from* Him than *to* Him. If we had even the slightest understanding of God's heart for us we would do just the opposite. We would run fearlessly with all our might back to His embrace, for He loves us, He *likes* us, even in our weakness, our sin, and our rebellion.

ENJOYED, EVEN IN OUR IMMATURITY

Even after returning, many believers fail to comprehend how overjoyed God is, how He enjoys their presence even as they are craving His. These people grow slowly in their Christian walk, holding God at arm's length. When they inevitably stumble, as all toddlers do, they brace themselves for the stern correction of God that they've been conditioned to expect. It pains God's heart to see them cower away from Him, because He knows they haven't come to understand that He loves them even in their immaturity. However, it is in responding to God's love in this immature weakness that ultimately brings us to maturity. We can only grit our teeth and resist sin for so long. We are truly transformed and able to turn away from sin when we finally get rooted in the true gospel: we can do nothing either to earn or to disqualify ourselves from the grace God has given us.

We all battle with various areas in our lives. Many people assume that each time they stumble in spiritual immaturity, God reacts as though they are in rebellion. This is not the truth. There is a vast difference between rebellion and spiritual immaturity. Thankfully, God knows the difference between the two—and He knows when we step into either. A spiritually immature person is sincere in their intent to obey the Lord and is frustrated by their own immaturity. While outwardly or to the undiscerning eye they may appear rebellious, inwardly they are very different. The spiritually immature believer continues to declare war on their failures and set their heart and soul against them, which in turn builds and creates in them the maturity that they lack. God actually enjoys them while they are still struggling in their immaturity and growing into maturity.

As we watch our children grow, we anticipate moments of immaturity. The reason two-year-olds are impatient has a lot to do with the fact that they're only two years old. When they throw a cup across the kitchen because they can't reach the goldfish, they aren't disqualified from the family or from their parents' affections. They are not excommunicated from the family. Immaturity becomes a teaching moment, not a relational breakdown. The parents know that it will not always be as it is at the moment; after all, their toddler is growing up.

Now, if parents can recognize that their child is growing up, cannot God recognize the issues of our own immaturity much more clearly? Does God have less desire or a more limited perspective than we do? Somehow we imagine that God does not really understand the dilemmas of our immaturity. But stop for a moment and consider what is obvious. The Father has a far superior love than even the best earthly parents. He can see all the issues, and can therefore enjoy us in a profound way even while we are growing up spiritually. Jesus even compared the Father's relationship with us to that between a parent and child.

> "If a son asks for bread from any father among you, will he give him a stone? Or if he asks for a fish, will he give him a serpent instead of a fish?...If you then, being evil, know how to give good gifts to your children, how much more will your heavenly Father give the Holy Spirit to those who ask Him!" (Luke 11:11-13)

The point is clearly made—no one knows how to parent us or shepherd our development like God does. His wisdom far surpasses that of any earthly parent. Our heavenly Father sees us in our immaturity and enjoys us as we grow. The Lord loves spiritual two-year-olds, even if they're living in fifty-five-year-old bodies. Understanding that God can and does enjoy us even in our immaturity fundamentally changes the way we view Him. Every day we can be assured that He enjoys us. When we make immature mistakes, He uses them as teaching opportunities without putting us on probation or sending us to some purgatory-style sin bin to mull over how wicked we have been. Even as He teaches us through the situation, He is expressing His love.

> For whom the LORD loves He corrects, just as a father the son in whom he delights. (Proverbs 3:12)

We often mistake correction for rejection. When God corrects or disciplines us, He does not reject us. Rather, He corrects us because He so desires us. We must make a clear distinction between loving correction and punishment that rejects. When we do, we realize a vital truth about our God, that He likes us. The opposite of the assurance that we are enjoyed is the fear of rejection and the trauma of shame, which are two sides of one coin. Rejection and shame are the most powerful negative human emotions and the most common strongholds of the mind. They cripple people emotionally. Every human being struggles with different degrees of rejection. We can be emotionally drained and even devastated if we believe God is rejecting and shaming us or if we believe the same about those we love. But to feel enjoyed by the Father and cherished by Jesus overpowers rejection and shame. Without the revelation of divine enjoyment we are much more vulnerable to Satan and his traps to answer this longing in a false way. This deception is the seedbed for many false religions that lure people into guilt and useless striving to escape the stigma of shame.

As God assures us of His enjoyment, the strongholds of rejection and shame are dismantled. A spiritual pleasure is released in our souls that is second to none. Oh, the assurance that we are delighted in, enjoyed, and longed for! With this we can rest on the inside. God likes us so much, in fact, that He is able to balance this amazing relational dynamic with His children: *every* believer is God's favorite. Most Christians will acknowledge having felt the love of God, but the idea of each one being His favorite may seem a bit far-fetched. How can any of us have multiple favorites? Doesn't the very meaning of the word *favorite* imply a single individual?

GOD'S FAVORITE

Perhaps in the limitations of human relationships there can only be room for one favorite, but we're dealing with a God who loves in a greater dimension than we can comprehend. He literally loves us in the same way He loves His own Son, the second Person of His being (John 15:9). Jesus revealed this astounding concept to His disciples. He said that He loved them in the way the Father loved Him. Think about it for a minute—how deeply does the Father love Jesus? What does the God who is love feel about the God who is love? This is how Jesus feels about us, making each of God's people His favorite. You are beloved of God or, as I like to say, you are God's favorite. Jesus longs for you. You have not been given salvation simply for the sake of a passport to heaven. Jesus actually likes talking to you, He enjoys the thought of ruling with you. He likes you. He enjoys your company. He appreciates you as a person, even as a friend.

This truth may be difficult for you to believe, but other followers of Jesus have seized on this very idea without reservation. The apostle John often referred to himself as having this special, unique relationship with Jesus. John referred to himself as "the one Jesus loved." Imagine presenting yourself before God in worship as the one God loves. This is precisely how John saw himself. Remember, John wrote the gospel of John. Notice how he referred to himself in the narrative.

> Jesus saw...the disciple [John] whom He loved standing by... (John 19:26)
>
> She ran to Simon Peter, and to the other disciple [John], whom Jesus loved, and said... (John 20:2)
>
> That disciple whom Jesus loved [John] said to Peter... (John 21:7)
>
> Then Peter...saw the disciple [John] whom Jesus loved... (John 21:20)
>
> Now there was leaning on Jesus' bosom one of His disciples [John], whom Jesus loved. (John 13:23)

It would be easy to read this and think, "John had some nerve! Didn't he know that believers down through the years would read this?" This idea of being God's favorite is vastly different from some notion of superiority over other believers. In calling himself "the disciple Jesus loved," John wasn't displaying exceptional nerve, *he was demonstrating personal revelation*. John understood that Jesus' heart burned for John when they spoke together. This was not a king speaking to the masses, this was an infinitely personal God speaking to His favorite friend.

Being God's favorite did not mean John was better than others. Instead, it pointed to the supreme love of God, a God uniquely able to love individuals to the utmost. This is the place in which disillusionment is conquered and holy zeal is awakened. We go the Father to find out who we are instead of going to other people. Whose opinion really matters? It is here that we understand our identity, here that we understand who we are.

In realizing that we are God's favorite, we gain specific advantages in the battle for our hearts, our minds, our peace, our joy. The enemy accuses us on two fronts. First, he tells us that we're rejected by God rather than beloved. Second, he says we're not sincere in our love of God because our love is weak. The enemy tells us that our weak love is pitiable and diluted, and even that it is completely false. When we finally understand that neither of these precepts is true, the enemy loses his ability to accuse us in these areas. We are able to believe that God is near, not far away. We understand that though our love may be weak, it is certainly growing—and even now we are enjoyed and desired by God.

We must understand that we are beloved of God. Abiding in confidence in love before God is a necessary foundation for walking in intimacy with Him. This requires living in the reality of our "belovedness" before God. To be beloved by God is to have confidence in His love and His ability to meet us where we are.

David is another one who understood he was the beloved of God (Psalm 60:5). David knew what it was to be God's favorite. For the greater part of his life he was recklessly abandoned to God. At the same time, there were episodes in his life when he was simply reckless. His passions brought forth the purest worship lyrics of all time and caused him to make some of the worst mistakes recorded in the Bible. Yet, in all this, his revelation of being God's beloved was foundational to his trusting and praising God. Even in his weakness he knew that he was totally forgiven, delighted in, and absolutely dear to God. It was knowing these truths that enabled him to establish and maintain a deep and unshakable intimacy with God.

David understood that God did not see his spiritual immaturity as rebellion. He knew that the Lord does not focus on outward appearance, but sees the movements of the heart. Samuel prophesied this truth over David when he anointed him as Israel's king. David went on to build his life and reign on the basis of this revelation.

> The Lord said, "...for the Lord does not see as man sees; for man looks at the outward appearance, but the Lord looks at the heart." (1 Samuel 16:7)

Through this Scripture we glimpse how differently God evaluates compared with man. God's assessments are not based on human ability, but on the movements of our heart before and toward Him. David had an unusual ability to receive God's mercy because of his confidence in it.

> I have trusted in Your mercy; my heart shall rejoice in Your salvation... (Psalm 13:5)

As a practical example, at the height of tensions with Saul, David fled to Ziklag, a small town in the land of Israel's enemies, the Philistines. Eventually David found favor with the Philistines and was allowed to live with them for sixteen months. But it was a place of compromise. David finally repented, left Ziklag and returned to Israel. We can see David's heart in the prayer he offered to God when he left that place of compromise: he still knew God delighted in him, even during that difficult season.

> He delivered me because He delighted in me. (Psalm 18:19)

If God counted our wrongs against us without showing mercy, we would never last long in a relationship with Him. The very nature of walking with God hinges on His kindness and grace to us.

> If You, Lord, should mark iniquities, O Lord, who could stand? But there is forgiveness with You, that You may be feared. (Psalm 130:3)

David knew God's love, and because of this knowledge he grasped God's mercy. Mercy is granted to our friends. God saw David as a friend. Knowing David's struggles and failures, it is encouraging to see how God's affections were poured out on him, even in times of his spiritual immaturity.

David had a free spirit because he knew that his deepest desires could not be obstructed by man. If our internal life in God is where our greatest longings are fulfilled, no man can block them and all human threats and temptations for favor are minimized. We must "get into" this vast ocean of endless divine love, in which the enjoyment of God is of paramount importance. The inexhaustible sea of divine love is declared in these passages, as well as others.

> ...that you...may be able to comprehend... what is the width and length and depth and height—to know the love of Christ which passes knowledge... (Ephesians 3:17-19)

> The Lord has appeared of old to me, saying: "Yes, I have loved you with an everlasting love; therefore with lovingkindness I have drawn you." (Jeremiah 31:3)

Over the last seven years, the International House of Prayer has hosted hundreds of interns, many of whom join our staff as full-time intercessory missionaries. One thing I enjoy most in being around so many young interns is watching them fall in love. When a young couple falls in love, something interesting invariably happens: their schedules converge. They miraculously find themselves in the prayer room together, in the coffee shop together, or in the case of some of our NightWatch staff, standing in the parking lot watching the sunrise together. Love draws hearts into proximity to one another. This is similar to when we begin to comprehend that God enjoys being with us!

> "Father, I desire that they also whom You gave Me
> may be with Me where I am, that they may behold
> My glory which You have given Me." (John 17:24)

In this prayer, Jesus revealed the deep groan of His heart that He has carried from eternity past: He voiced His desire for mankind to be with Him where He is. The very centerpiece of God, the Father's eternal plan, is that He would dwell with us forever. Our longing to be enjoyed is matched by His longing to enjoy us. Out of all the created order, the human heart has been given a unique gift: the capacity for affection. This capacity has not even been released to angels—only to human beings. In His infinite wisdom, the Bridegroom God decided to only share the realm of affection with human beings.

God has orchestrated the ideal circumstances in this age to produce the greatest amount and most intense level of love in the human heart. When asked on the last day about Jesus' leadership over our lives, we will declare, "His dealings with me were perfect. He was so tender in the way He led me. I longed to give Him pleasure, and He found it in me." In that moment, His desire will be fully realized. And we will find our fulfillment completely and perfectly in Him.

CHAPTER TWO

The Longing for Fascination

Right now, even this very moment, a drama is taking place around the throne of God. This drama has been going on since long before the earth was created. The living creatures, the seraphim (which literally means "burning ones"), gaze upon God's throne night and day with adoration and fascination (Revelation 4:8; Isaiah 6:2-3). They peer into the mysteries of God and are overwhelmed and awestruck. When the prophet Isaiah witnessed these burning ones before God's throne, the experience left him speechless. When finally able to describe this encounter, he gave us insight into what it is like to view the beauty of God up close.

> I saw the Lord sitting on a throne, high and lifted up...above it stood seraphim; each one had six wings: with two he covered his face, with two he covered his feet, and with two he flew. And one cried to another and said: "Holy, holy, holy is the Lord of hosts!" (Isaiah 6:1-3)

The seraphim, the beings nearest the throne, continually bow and cover their eyes in response to the awesomeness of God's beauty. As the powerful impact of the revelation of God races through them, they bow and rise up again. They cry,

"Holy, holy, holy," which means, "Transcendent beauty, transcendent beauty, transcendent beauty!" They are undone with the incessant fascination and exhilarating worship; they never exhaust the endless ocean of God's beauty, never reach the limit of this eternal expanse. This undeviating fascination is what humanity was made for. We, the redeemed, can experience it in great measure in this life and in its fullest measure for all eternity.

The fascinating God created us with a need to be fascinated. In every human spirit there is a craving to marvel. We long to be filled with endless wonder. God placed a sense of wondering at the core of our design. The secular entertainment industry has identified this longing and targeted it commercially. Even at its best, however, secular entertainment is no match for the fascinating God of the universe. No eye has seen, no mind has conceived what He has in store for those who love Him (1 Corinthians 2:9). Our highest imagination cannot perceive the fullness of that which will leave us awestruck throughout the eternal ages—the beauty of God Himself. When we are not fascinated with Him we become bored, spiritually dull, and spiritually passive. To a heart not living in fascination with God, the substitutes of money, drugs, alcohol, and immorality are far more tempting, though ultimately they are completely unsatisfying.

It is the nature of mankind to wonder and to explore, to uncover what is hidden, all in hopes of a new discovery. One thing all scientists and inventors have in common is their insatiable curiosity. The great scientific breakthroughs of history were the fruit of such curiosity. As children, men like Albert Einstein and the Wright brothers were constantly interested in how things worked. Einstein saw his first compass at age five. As the needle swung to the north no matter which direction it was pointed, the boy who would one day pen the theory of relativity stood amazed. Later he said this experience led him to believe there

---

[1] American Institute of Physics' historical exhibit on Albert Einstein: The Formative Years. More information at http://www.aip.org/history/einstein/early1.htm.

was "something behind things, something deeply hidden."[1]

Mankind has always searched for that "something behind things, something deeply hidden." It drives us to explore, it drives us to wonder, and it is intended to drive us to God, because it is a longing He put in us. As with the other cravings He places in our heart, He always provides the ultimate and eternal fulfillment. He designed us with a desire for fascination and offers Himself as the satisfaction of our desire.

King David had the same sort of curiosity as the great minds of our day. He received a glimpse of God's beauty and charted the course for his life using that as his guide. We don't know exactly when or how it happened, but he later wrote that seeking God's beauty became a lifelong fascination for him: "One thing I desire…all the days of my life, to behold the beauty of the Lord" (Psalm 27:4). For a man with the whole kingdom of Israel under his leadership, these are strong words. David was one of the most powerful men on the planet at the height of his reign, yet encountering God was the great focus of his life. The palaces, the wives, the horses, and the armies paled in comparison to that one thing, and he made it his life's ambition to get one more look…and one more…and one more.

FASCINATION FULFILLED IN GOD

Satan did not invent the idea of pleasure. He counterfeited it and uses it to destroy the human heart. God has granted us the capacity to sense pleasure—physical, emotional, and mental pleasure. But the most profound of the God-given pleasures is found in the realm of spiritual pleasure. Spiritual pleasures resonate in us at a deeper level than any of the others. When God the Holy Spirit reveals God the Son to us, our spirit resonates within us. This is the greatest experience of delight and satisfaction available to the human race. This revelation of God *by* God allows us to experience "divine entertainment." Only God is equipped to satisfy in such a way. The Holy Spirit will take the things of Jesus and give them to us: "He will take of what is

Mine and declare it to you" (John 16:14).

God points us toward a day when all this wondering and searching will be fulfilled in its totality. Our longing for fascination will be completely realized. Isaiah 4:2 is one of my favorite Old Testament prophecies for God's people at the end of the age. God promised to cause the human heart to be awestruck with Jesus, that "In that day, the Branch of the LORD [Jesus] shall be beautiful and glorious" (Isaiah 4:2). Five times in Scripture, the prophets call the Messiah the "Branch of the Lord," and it is a term used for the Messiah in His humanity. Of course, this is Jesus, the second Person of the Trinity. Isaiah was writing of the beauty of God being revealed in the person of Jesus to the nations of earth. This revelation of Jesus will fascinate the hearts of God's people.

Isaiah gave another well-known prophecy of Jesus' beauty being seen by all: "Your eyes will see the King in His beauty" (Isaiah 33:17). Jesus is beautiful beyond comprehension, and there is coming a day when we shall see Him in all His revealed beauty. A lifetime of longing—seventy, eighty, a hundred years—will suddenly be fulfilled as we gaze upon our Maker and Redeemer. As the seraphim attest, we will never grow bored with gazing upon Him. What begins in initial fascination will grow and develop. What all the abilities of mankind could not aspire to do, God will do in fullness for all eternity—He will *truly* fascinate our hearts. He will put Himself on display—the essence of beauty, the perfection of splendor and magnificence. Jesus' name is called "Wonderful" because He alone can fill the hearts of His people with wonder. The eternal confession of the redeemed will be, "He is Wonderful."

> For unto us a Child is born, unto us a Son is given...
> His name will be called Wonderful... (Isaiah 9:6)

The pleasures of God and the comprehension of His majesty go far beyond our ability to imagine. Even here on earth we regularly see things we couldn't have dreamed would be so beautiful. It's not uncommon to hear people, who have heard about it for decades, standing on the rim of the Grand Canyon, say, "I had no idea..." If an earthly canyon, a creation of God, can inspire such awe, then how can we even begin to imagine the beauty of that Creator Himself?

OVERCOMING SPIRITUAL BOREDOM

It is God's plan and pleasure to unlock the divine treasure chest and reveal the beauty of His Son to fulfill our longing for fascination. Even now the way is being made clear for us to see the beauty of Jesus. The Holy Spirit is described as searching or discerning the deep and hidden things of God's being in order that He may reveal them to us. Invited by the Spirit, guided by the glory of God evident through His creation and His Word, we have the privilege of searching out and discovering an infinite God.

> But as it is written: "Eye has not seen, nor ear heard, nor have entered into the heart of man the things which God has prepared for those who love Him." But God has revealed them to us through His Spirit. For the Spirit searches all things, yes, the deep things of God. For what man knows the things of a man except the spirit of the man which is in him? Even so no one knows the things of God except the Spirit of God. Now we have received, not the spirit of the world, but the Spirit who is from God, that we might know the things that have been freely given to us by God. (1 Corinthians 2:9-12)

We have a beautiful God beckoning us to encounter His beauty, but we must understand that it takes time and energy to begin plumbing the depths of God. It takes time and energy to pray and fast and study Scripture. Those who expend all their energies in their jobs and ministries, and then in pursuit of entertainment and recreation, quickly find themselves depleted. Many of God's people, well-intentioned people, find themselves without the time or energy to fast, pray, or read Scripture. We cannot throw ourselves headlong into a hundred pursuits at the expense of searching out and experiencing God. We cannot over-saturate our souls with activity. This can only lead to a dull spirit.

In his book *The Evidential Power of Beauty*, Thomas Dubay traces the signature of God through the physical world. Ranging from the cosmic rotation of planets to the makeup of Earth's atmosphere, through the wonders of biology on the molecular level and down to the behavior of atomic particles, Dubay sees the revelation of the beauty of God. To read this book with an open heart is to marvel at the intentionality of God and His amazing commitment to beauty. He makes things beautiful because He *is* beauty. Since His creation speaks of Him, to encounter these tokens of beauty is to catch a sideways glance at the beautiful God. Consider this, and then imagine the things of God that will exhilarate the human heart throughout eternity.

One of the great problems in the Body of Christ today is that of spiritual boredom. Many churches are made up of people who have been inundated with entertainment and recreation. Pastors feel compelled to compete with the things that grapple for the attention of their flocks. Listening to the Lord becomes secondary to figuring out how they're going to hold the atrophied attention of people demanding an instant shot of stimulation. A night out at the latest blockbuster movie moves us to tears, but the worship service the next morning does nothing for us, dulled as we are into expecting drive-thru fulfillment, rather than devoting ourselves to eternal fascination. It is tragic how we invest what limited passion we have in things that simply do not satisfy.

FALSE FASCINATION IN ENTERTAINMENT

This holy fascination, the hunger for the revelation of Einstein's "something deeply hidden," has been placed within each one of us by God. Mankind has worked hard to fill it with other things.

The Greeks had their theaters and the Romans their coliseums. Today, our suburbs are dotted with multiplex theaters, temples of false fascination. Unable to reproduce the celestial beauty of God, the heart of man has always reverted to earthly entertainment. America is unique among world cultures in that the entertainment industry commands a major portion of our economy and a greater portion of our time. It is the economics of supply and demand on an emotional level, but in this case the supply does not begin to truly fulfill the demand. Today's blockbuster is forgotten in a week. We alternate between being fascinated by and bored with entertainment. That which we thought we could not do without becomes suddenly unsatisfying, even repulsive.

Scripture tells us the story of Amnon, who was sinfully fascinated with Tamar. Completely convinced that she would fulfill his needs, he plotted and planned until he had a moment alone with her and then forced himself upon her. In the human sense, he got exactly what he wanted, but the nature of pursuing earthly pleasure is graphically revealed in what happened immediately afterwards.

> Then Amnon hated her exceedingly, so that the hatred with which he hated her was greater than the love with which he had loved her. (2 Samuel 13:15)

The very object of Amnon's desire, the thing he thought he craved so much, became repulsive to him. She was yesterday's blockbuster, last week's hit song, a means to sating his lust that was no longer fulfilling, and so he cast her aside. We do the same thing with all manner of entertainment today. Once it's experienced, it's over. And we feel all the more dissatisfied for it.

While I am not against entertainment, I am gravely concerned about the primacy of place it takes in our society. As we increase our intake of earthly entertainment we dull our capacity to be fascinated by God. It's not that we don't want to see God, we just can't find Him among the barrage of information to which we're exposing ourselves. One does not have to be a spiritual giant to recognize the long-term implications of gorging on earthly entertainment while neglecting and dulling our ability to be fascinated with God Himself. It would be hard to find many in the Body of Christ who feel positive about the entertainment culture in which we live.

We must likewise acknowledge the segment of entertainment that is more than just unsatisfying, but overtly destructive. As we attempt to fulfill our innate desires through movies, music and other forms of entertainment, we are touched in deeply personal places. We open up our innermost being to ultimately damaging messages, only to find ourselves frustrated, broken, and abused by these forms of entertainment. One example might be the young man who feeds himself a steady diet of music that reflects ungodly attitudes towards women. Unknowingly, that young man is setting the stage for a failed marriage by allowing those messages to form who he is on the inside. By exposing our hearts to some forms of so-called entertainment, we feed our souls with attitudes about people and relationships that can take years to undo.

Rather than acknowledge their hunger for fascination, and accept that God is the answer to that hunger, some people turn away from God all together. They blame their problems on the desire for fascination itself, rather than on the unhealthy way in which they've fulfilled their desire. This is something akin to repenting for breathing. We were made to breathe. We were made to be fascinated. The problem is not with the desire, but with attempting to fulfill the desire in a wrong way, which then brings frustration. Trying to scourge oneself from the sin of breathing will have the same success rate as attempting to escape fascination. By ridding themselves of entertainment, by turning off their televisions and avoiding movies, they successfully insulate themselves from certain unhealthy fascinations. But this purging of influence will never fill the void remaining in their hearts. While earthly entertainment may have been junk food, at least it was food. They may not have been healthy in partaking of it, but at least they weren't hungry. After a few weeks or even months of this total lack of fascination, they realize they're terminally bored. They removed the useless influence but failed to replace it with being fascinated by God. Confused, they plop themselves back on the couch and grab the remote control, telling themselves that the whole thing was a legalistic phase.

It is a prime trick of the enemy to leverage the God-given desire for fascination to entice us into actions that end up dulling our perception of the fascinating beauty of God. Whether it's entertainment, a sense of power, or another cheap replacement, we find ourselves exhausted with our pursuit of everything except the face of God. The apostle Paul wrote of his earlier fascination with his religious crusade as a persecutor of Christians. He said his zeal drove him—until he had an encounter on the Damascus road that stopped him in his tracks.

> I also count all things loss for the excellence of the knowledge of Christ Jesus my Lord, for whom I have suffered the loss of all things, and count them as rubbish, that I may gain Christ. (Philippians 3:8)

The lesson from Paul is clear. No matter what is fascinating our hearts now, it is far less valuable, profound, and lasting than the superior pleasures of Jesus. The drive for position or entertainment will fall by the wayside as we begin to see the beauty of Christ Jesus. We have a never-ending capacity and longing to be filled with amazement and for wonder to touch our spirit, and God has a never-ending capacity to fill it. He has all that it takes to keep us energized for billions of years, and even then we will find we are only in the shallows of the vast ocean of His beauty.

God is orchestrating a divine revolution to turn people's pursuit of fascination upside-down. He is revealing Himself as the One who truly satisfies. At the end of the age, God's people will be more fascinated with Jesus than at any other time in history (Revelation 22:17). They will be enthralled by what they see in Jesus. It will change their very beings as they are moved by the beauty of God on His throne. For the first time in their lives, they will sing with full understanding, "Great and marvelous are Your works, Lord God Almighty" (Revelation 15:2-

3). God will release an impartation of beauty to people whose lives have become smoldering ash heaps of broken humanity. In His first public teaching, Jesus clearly laid out what He came to do. Intrinsic to His mission on earth was bringing beauty to the downtrodden. Isaiah prophesied, and Jesus later quoted:

> "The Spirit of the Lord GOD is upon Me, because the LORD has anointed Me to preach good tidings to the poor...to proclaim liberty to the captives... to proclaim the acceptable year of the LORD...to give them beauty for ashes, the oil of joy for mourning..." (Isaiah 61:1-3)

It is not uncommon to find people who have reduced their lives to rubble. Usually the pursuit of earthly fascination has made a significant contribution. Having been created to marvel at the glory of God, many people instead live bored, aimless, and destructive lives. They have no revelation of God. They graduate from high school full of promise, and fifteen years later find themselves spiritually bored, disconnected, and isolated from God's people, addicted to pornography, alcohol, or making money, and in the ruins of a second or third marriage. Sure, they have reasons for their addictions, boredom, and ruined family relationships—they usually center around unmet expectations. Their God-given desire to be fascinated was never met by this or that job, this or that church or ministry, even this or that spouse. Now they sit in an absolute wreck of a situation. But God says that their current reality does not need to be their lifelong or eternal one.

Jesus came to offer an incredible trade—beauty for ashes. God looks at the ashes nobody wants and says, "Don't throw them away! I want them! Give them to Me, and I will give My beauty in exchange for the useless mess into which their lives have devolved." God Himself is the alternate reality for those who are broken and beaten down. In the revelation of His Son, Jesus, a way is made for people to find joy and the fulfillment of their heart's longing. Their lives can be changed through progressive encounters with the beauty of God as seen in the face of Jesus (2 Corinthians 4:6).

THE BEAUTY OF GOD AS OUR OCCUPATION

The beauty of the Lord is more than just a divine exchange program, although that's one very real facet. God wants to do much more than simply trade our messes for His majesty. The beauty of the Lord has been ordained as the occupation of God's people. He wants us to be fascinated by His beauty on a daily basis now and for all of eternity. We have earthly promises and mandates to be fulfilled in our lifetimes. Some of us will pastor congregations, some will feed and minister to the poor, others will serve as conduits of funds to further God's purposes. While these are God-ordained assignments for this life, none of these mandates will last forever. In those roles there is a God-given measure of satisfaction, but at some point those assignments will be complete. As immortal souls operating in a mortal world, we must look for something eternal to fascinate hearts that are designed to live *forever*. And we must begin to cultivate it now.

I've said a lot about both entertainment and earthly assignments. I truly don't want to dismiss the validity of some of these things. It is not that they all are invalid or evil; they are simply inferior to the superior pleasures of God. God's strategy is to liberate people from believing the lie that their temporal assignments are all there is in life. We're called to something bigger than *less than*.

Anyone who's ever watched a five-year-old fight sleep knows why they're fighting. They don't hate sleep, they're just afraid they're going to miss something. They'll run in circles, sing songs, throw a temper tantrum, or pick a fight with a sibling to avoid falling asleep. They are convinced that the moment they do, the real party will start without them: mom and dad will roll back the rug, a band will appear from nowhere, and party guests will arrive. Of course, mom and dad have no intention of doing this, but to the child, the fear is real. Most people never outgrow this. They live with the fear of missing something. They can't imagine coming to the office and hearing talk of a movie they have not seen or a song they have not heard. They hunger for experience and expend a huge amount of energy staying current on the temporal, inferior pleasures of life, while missing out on the superior pleasures of God in the process. They never have time to be captivated by the beauty of God because they are consumed with the potential of what they might become on their own.

What is true in the realm of entertainment is also true in the realm of ministry or secular employment. People lie awake at night and dedicate themselves to wondering, "What if I miss my big chance? Will I be there to take the phone call that puts me on the map?" It may very well be that God does want you to be on the map, that He does have thoughts of promoting you in people's eyes. But I can promise you this: all those promotions are very much like entertainment; at the end of the day, they are still inferior pleasures. They are still *less than*, and without the fascination of God, they are ultimately nothing.

People who chase entertainment or positions do not have the energy to persevere in their pursuit of the beauty of God. There just aren't enough hours in the day. If they really want to fulfill the longing of their heart for fascination, they must make the same determination David did, "to pursue this one thing… to behold the beauty of God." Fortunately for all of us, this is exactly the opportunity God is looking for. He has the answer for inferior pleasures. Throughout history, God has woven an elegant story of redemption to cause us to marvel, to gaze upon Him and His ways in fascination, awe, and wonder. More importantly, this story is moving rapidly toward a crescendo at the end of the age—the unveiling of the beauty of His Son. It will be His ultimate expression of giving beauty for ashes.

God did not intend for us to grit our teeth in order to prevail against a lifetime of inferior pleasures. He knew that willpower alone couldn't pull us through, so He created superior pleasures. Pleasure is what motivates us to abandon the lesser things and give ourselves to Jesus. God revealing God to the human spirit is the most exhilarating experience in the universe. This "divine entertainment" causes earthly entertainment and human accomplishment to melt away in obvious inferiority. As we progressively see Him in all His glory and splendor, boredom ceases to be an issue.

The Bible says it is possible to satiate our desire for fascination in Jesus' beauty. When we make a commitment to holiness and set our hearts to pursue the greater pleasures of knowing Him, God makes us a promise—that *our eyes will see* the King in His beauty (Isaiah 33:17). Making a commitment to the Lord always has benefits. Making a commitment to pursue His beauty pays off in both the short and long term, as He fulfills our longings for fascination and increases our capacity for it at the same time. As beautiful as Jesus can be to us now (and, yes, Jesus really is enough to exceed all our expectations) we will receive more and more of His beauty in the days to come. He gives us a glimpse of this increasing revelation of beauty as a down payment of sorts, to say, "Pursue Me. I have superior pleasures that you will never find on earth, and even greater things in store for you in the coming age" (Matthew 6:31-34; Mark 10:29-30; Luke 18:29-30).

A satisfied, fascinated believer is a spiritually strong believer who lives with a special measure of protection from Satan's schemes. Many of the opportunities for sin that come their way are rejected, not because of some moral superiority over those who may fall for the same trick, but simply because the believer is preoccupied with the beauty of God and has no attention to give to lesser pleasures. The deceptions of the enemy are more quickly exposed for what they are: unsatisfying distractions from that which is truly fulfilling.

The beauty of God reaches its high point in the revelation of Jesus as our Bridegroom King. The overwhelming beauty of the Bridegroom King will ravish the end-time church, enabling her to suffer every kind of persecution and tribulation, and remain fervent in love (2 Thessalonians 1:3-12). Even in death, believers will fix their eyes solely upon the One who will soon split the sky with His appearing and destroy the enemy with His brightness (2 Thessalonians 2:8). The splendor-filled person of Jesus will be the focus of the saints at this time, and they will burn with a holy fascination as they gaze upon His unsurpassed beauty. This is one of the chief themes in the kingdom of God—the Lord's promise to unveil the beauty of Jesus in a unique way to the generation that will see His return.

Though most of the Church in the Western world has lost its wonder in God, the Lord will redress this great tragedy. The passive, stagnant, spiritually dull Western church will be awakened as God reveals Himself once again. He is even now releasing a new anointing on the Church, an enabling to perceive Jesus' beauty in order to answer the craving for awe and wonder. Within the bridal paradigm of the kingdom, God is revealing the beauty of Jesus as the Bridegroom God, making the inferior pleasures obsolete and communicating His own transcendent beauty in order to fascinate His end-time church.

Pornography, riches, and self-promotion have no appeal to a person fascinated with Christ Jesus. There is more to serving God than simply gritting your teeth and trying to avoid evil. Perceiving Jesus' beauty results in the supernatural strengthening of the inner man. Likewise, the political spirit that has been so prominent throughout church history will be conquered by only one thing: a holy preoccupation, a fascination with the beauty of Christ Jesus. Those with powerful ministries or open doors to government will see their auspicious position as secondary and proclaim, "I am captured by Jesus!"

Jesus Himself will rock the Church as the Holy Spirit unlocks the treasure trove of His glory and splendor. The Church will fall hopelessly in love with the Man Jesus, considering it their glory to give up everything to and for Him. The Father has chosen to enthrall the human heart through the most powerful weapon He has: unveiling the knowledge of Jesus through the power of the Holy Spirit.

People often say, "I don't have time for a devotional life in prayer and the Word of God." The reason they don't have time is that they don't know what God has in store for them as they wait before Him. A "devotional life" is not a bargaining chip to get God to pay attention. It is the way into pleasure, into His power, and into having an enthralled heart! In revealing His Son, God fascinates His people beyond anything they have ever known. This fascination serves as a holy protection mechanism from all the deceptions of the enemy, and it strengthens believers with a godly motivation to always reach toward the beauty that will remain when all else fades away.

CHAPTER THREE

The Longing for Beauty

Rhodes Scholar Christopher Morley was the founder and editor of the *Saturday Review of Literature*. He once said, "In every man's heart there is a secret nerve that answers to the vibrations of beauty." If this is true, if beauty is a desire common to humanity, would it exist only to be met in some eternal sense? The heart is a resonance chamber, a God-designed void created to be filled with and to reflect the beauty of God. And the beautiful God made His favorite creations to be beautiful. God's beauty emanates from His person and resonates within us. We reflect God's own beauty. We couldn't have created the beauty ourselves—we reflect His beauty.

BEAUTY IMPARTED, BEAUTY REVEALED

There is something in the human spirit that detests feeling ugly. We exert much energy and spend a great deal of time and money to fix the things about ourselves that we consider less than attractive. We powder, primp, comb, and cover whatever we can to appear our best. We long to be attractive and beautiful, and this longing is an expression of God's genius and personality. A beautiful God created us in such a way that we long to possess beauty, to be striking and engaging. We also long to perceive beauty, to gaze upon it. God will fully answer this longing in every one of its expressions beyond our wildest imaginations. We are all meant to feel beautiful before God and there is something powerful about those who genuinely do. When the Holy Spirit shows us what God is like and then shows us what we look like to God, something settles in our hearts, minds, and emotions. Our priorities and values change. The revelation of God's beauty has two dimensions to it: first, the beauty of Jesus as our Bridegroom, and second, the beauty of His Bride.

Don't think this is just a female thing: men give a different name to this same longing, and call it a desire to be *cool*. The impulse of the heart is the same, and has the same solution: the glorious news that the beauty God possesses is the very beauty He imparts to His people through redemption. His beauty is transferable to human beings through Jesus. The person who sets his heart to investigate this will find it a staggering concept! God imparts His beauty through redemption to formerly broken, hopeless, sin-ridden, even demonized, people.

This longing to be beautiful has a huge impact on how we structure our time and spend our money. Every day, millions of dollars and countless hours are spent in pursuit of physical beauty—hair is styled, clothes are selected, gym memberships are renewed, and diets are started, all in the pursuit of beauty. Most people pursue beauty at great lengths because of the unsettled, unhappy feeling they have when they feel ugly. We vigorously chase after beauty and resist that which seems imperfect. In seeking to answer this legitimate longing, our culture has cultivated an unhealthy, destructive obsession with physical appearance. The secular beauty industry has tapped into this longing in the human spirit and exploited it, creating frustration and self-loathing each step of the way. Advertising executives set the unrealistic standards by which we judge others and ourselves. Deceived by the airbrushed, computer-generated models in the magazines, and misled by arbitrarily-defined beauty, many people live frustrated lives, because, according to what we are told and sold, we are failing in the race to be beautiful.

It is perfectly acceptable to enhance one's physical appearance. However, there are healthy boundaries to this; more is not always better. The obsession with physical beauty is coming to a pinnacle in Western culture. People often become compulsive and stray outside the will of God, turning from utility to pursuit to overindulgence. Some people put an excessive amount of time and money into cosmetics, fashionable clothing, surgery, and fitness. Seeking for natural beauty outside the bounds of the grace of God can be harmful. To overlook godly boundaries is to end up with added pressure and troubles. Many sexual and eating disorders are, not surprisingly, linked to an obsession with natural beauty that goes beyond the protective boundaries of God's Word.

The vanity and frustration associated with beauty has led some to conclude that beauty itself is to blame, that the longing for beauty is synonymous with shallowness. Some religions have taken the longing to possess beauty and pronounced it evil. Nothing could be further from the truth—God Himself is the source of all true beauty. Right now, sitting on a throne in an unseen realm is a beautiful God. He is radiant in appearance. A pure river of life-giving water flows from under His throne and gets deeper and wider as it spreads. This is not a computer-generated image—there are no airbrush artists here—and this is not Hollywood. This is absolutely real—more real than anything we've ever experienced. As difficult as that is to imagine, it's even harder to realize that He wants to impart this same magnificent beauty to us. It's a part of His gift to us. His beauty, radiant and perfect, has been transferred to human beings through His Son, Jesus. In fact, that transfer is a key element of redemption, a part of His master plan.

HIS BEAUTY FOR OUR ASHES

In the last chapter, we looked at a passage in Isaiah describing God's plan for us:

> "The Spirit of the Lord GOD is upon Me, because
> the LORD has anointed Me to preach good tidings to
> the poor...to give them beauty for ashes..." (Isaiah
> 61:1-3)

Ashes are good for absolutely nothing. What does it mean to have ashes and why is it that we have them? They are the by-product and result of burning our passions on wrong things. Some believers' lives are like ash heaps even after they have known the Lord for many years. Most people don't realize how much they have lost by making sinful choices. They find themselves midway through life with nothing to show for it, or even worse, having accumulated a jumbled mess of wrecked relationships, disappointments, and debt. Regardless of how they arrived there, they come to a realization that they're sitting on an ash heap and they wonder, "What would anyone want with me? What I have done is so...ugly." Nobody wants our ashes. Nobody, that is, except God. And when He takes them, He will trade them for His beauty.

A significant purpose for which God sent Jesus to earth was to orchestrate a divine exchange on a level that is impossible for humans to orchestrate. Since the Creation, time after time, humans made choices that reduced their lives to ashes and rubble, to useless, worthless rubbish that nobody would want to possess. First in Eden, then at the tower of Babel, and again in the days of Noah, man repeatedly destroyed his own hope for future glory and beauty by his selfish acts. This pattern continues today and shows no sign of abating.

During the Reformation, Martin Luther revived evangelical Christianity as he accentuated the foundational spiritual, born-again experience. Unfortunately, decades of evangelical emphasis has left the Western church woefully out of tune with the fullness of redemption. We have concentrated on the legal benefits of salvation, but have almost resigned ourselves to living in the ash heap until we receive "a little cabin on the edge of glory, somewhere in the great beyond." In promising to exchange His beauty for our ashes, God says He will answer our core desire for beauty now, in this life, as well as for all eternity. Taking the mess we have made of our lives, He will give us the very thing our hearts were meant to possess—the beauty of God. When you became a believer, you weren't merely saved from hell. You were made to be beautiful and to show forth God's beauty to the rest of creation forever.

Because of an erroneous understanding of the desire for beauty, most people try to deny their attraction to it. We insist that we are not so shallow as to be distracted or even driven by beauty. At the same time, if offered any car, the one we would most likely choose would surely be the one described as "exotic"—the curve of the grille, the headlight cluster, and the sweeping profile that all scream *beauty*. We also choose suits by the cut of the cloth, how they transform our profiles into something magnetic, and by how luxurious we feel even when wearing them to the most mundane of occasions. Many of us search for a mate based on appearances, initially at least, and sometimes exclusively. Finding that this sort of beauty leaves us with vacant hearts, we rebel against the desire rather than the method we've used that led only to false answers. Some have gone too far and disavowed every association with natural beauty.

MANIFESTATION OF INNER BEAUTY

Something happens when believers realize that their yearnings for what is beautiful are truly God-designed. Rather than continue in denial about their yearning for beauty, they begin to look to God for the fulfillment of that yearning. In that moment, they become something more than they were the moment before. It is as if a door swings open in their heart. They become aware of beauty in their own life that is a deposit for things to come. The inner beauty of God manifests itself in us in a number of different ways. He changes our very countenance. Spiritual or inner beauty leaves tokens of physical beauty in this age by lighting up our countenance and changing our personality. In contrast, many sicknesses are related to a fearful and angry disposition as well as the ugliness of bitterness and pride. These negative attitudes *greatly* affect our bodies, even to the point of changing our physical expression. Peter wrote of the inner beauty of God having a profound effect on how people present themselves to one another.

> Do not let your adornment be merely outward... rather let it be the hidden person of the heart, with the incorruptible beauty of a gentle and quiet spirit, which is very precious in the sight of God. (1 Peter 3:3-4)

God will make us physically beautiful in the age to come, but having a bright spirit affects us in this age as well. It is limited but very real. When our spirit is beautified even our outward person is touched in the power of that beauty. A person who has a radiant spirit of righteousness has a different look about them. We've all had the experience of meeting someone who was physically beautiful but had a harsh or arrogant manner. It doesn't take long before we don't even consider that person attractive—their physical attributes fall by the wayside because they lack inner beauty. Scratch the surface of some physically beautiful people and you'll find an unattractive core. Likewise, we often meet people who may not get a second look on the street, but because of their gentle spirit they become beautiful to us. They radiate beauty from within. This inner beauty is part of the bigger inheritance of God's beauty we receive in part even now. Believers and nonbelievers alike are drawn like magnets to a gentle person who reflects the beauty of God. Moses prayed that the beauty of the Lord would be made apparent *through* His people. He wrote,

> Let the beauty of the LORD our God be upon us...
> (Psalm 90:17)

Why does God do this? What motivation could a divine King possibly have to share His beauty with His subjects? The answer is almost counterintuitive. The study of other world religions reveals that most represent their supposed deities as more interested in receiving alms from and controlling their followers than in actually benefiting them. One of the many things that makes the true God stand out so far above the false ones is His promise to make us beautiful with His own beauty. It is an expression of His affection and pleasure.

> For the LORD takes pleasure in His people; He will
> beautify the humble with salvation. (Psalm 149:4)

God takes pleasure in you. Take a moment and personalize that sentence, then read it out loud. *God takes pleasure in me.* That's a hard concept for many people: a God who takes pleasure in His people. Far from being stoic, His heart is warmed by the very people who come to Him for help. He takes great joy in beautifying them.

Feeling beautiful is not natural for most people. Even those who are attractive often claim and believe that no one thinks they are. Most fathers have had at least a few of those conversations through the bathroom door: "Daddy, I can't go to school today. I'm ugly!" While that child may be very attractive, at some level they feel their every flaw is magnified a hundred times. In the same way, most of us do not feel attractive when we stand before God. Wrong actions and attitudes run through our minds and all we see is the contrast between His holiness and our sin. So the idea of a beautiful God who makes us beautiful fundamentally changes how we interact with God and with other people. If He thinks we're beautiful—well, then it doesn't really matter if others agree or not! The King gazes upon us and likes what He sees!

> The King will greatly desire your beauty; because He
> is your Lord, worship Him. (Psalm 45:11)
>
> I am my beloved's, and his desire is toward me.
> (Song of Solomon 7:10)

When, instead of feeling ugly and hypocritical, a man or woman feels beautiful before God, something powerful is released. They become free of their own self-imposed shackles. The things that bound them to guilt and despair begin to fall away, as they see themselves as part of the Bride of the Holy One. Because He only surrounds Himself with beauty, being desired by God mandates that we are, in reality, truly beautiful.

His work in developing our beauty on this side of glory is astounding. It is nothing short of amazing to hear of His bringing beauty from the ashes of people's lives. In almost every church you will find testimonies of restored marriages, prodigals coming home, and people with the ability to stand confidently before God because of what He has done in their lives. Though all these testimonies may be true, the good news is that they do not even begin to represent the fullness of the beauty of God. There are ramifications far beyond this earthly life. The beauty we grow into in this life has continuity and significant magnification in the age to come; it gets bigger and better, and it is directly related to our lives on earth right now.

THE VAST SUBJECT OF OUR BEAUTY IN GOD

God's beauty in us is a vast subject. There is physical beauty and spiritual beauty, there is temporal beauty in this age, and there is eternal beauty in the age to come. You will possess physical beauty beyond the angels. Let there be no doubt: the Godhead is the main celestial attraction, but when He unveils His ultimate plan to present a beautiful Bride to Himself, the angels will gather at the balconies of heaven and shake their heads in wonder. You will be physically, emotionally, and spiritually beautiful forever because of Jesus. You will have a beautiful face, body, mind, and heart. Yes, you will be stunningly beautiful forever. In your resurrected body, you will possess a physical beauty for billions of years that will far surpass anything you can think of now. The beautiful God has already planned this from beginning to end.

He's been working on this plan for a long time. When God raised Jesus from the dead, He designed a body for Jesus that was unlike anything ever seen or imagined. It was both physically and spiritually beautiful. After Jesus was raised from the dead, He had the ability to walk through walls, yet He had the capacity to enjoy a breakfast of fish with His friends (John 20:26 and 21:12-15). His glorified body was the perfect melding of the spiritual and physical realms, allowing Jesus to partake of the best of both worlds. He has a body for each of us that is just like His. Our resurrected bodies will be the best that God can create, unable to be improved upon. At the second coming, Jesus will combine the natural realm with the supernatural realm (Ephesians 1:10; Revelation 21:1-2). Our bodies will be made with all the capacities necessary to express the glory and beauty of God in this new environment.

> He will transform the body of our humble condition into the likeness of His glorious body, by the power that enables Him to subject everything to Himself. (Philippians 3:21, HCSB)

> ...when He is revealed, we shall be like Him, for we shall see Him. (1 John 3:2)

LIGHT AND GLORY

Our eternal bodies will have the same supernatural properties and abilities that Jesus' body has. For example, Jesus wears garments of beautiful light; therefore, we shall as well.

> ...who cover Yourself with light as with a garment... (Psalm 104:2)

Jesus is the master communicator. He was able to speak in layers of truth that allowed the hearer to understand His point and yet continue to unravel and discover new meaning in what He was saying for years to come. One such example is when He said, "You are the light of the world" (Matthew 5:14). He was speaking of believers being beacons here in this age, but He was also referring to the future. He was speaking of the day when the saints would be made like Him, the One who lights up the New Jerusalem and the new earth as well (Revelation 21:23). The people of God in the New Jerusalem will also release God's light. The best computer models of twenty-first-century physics laboratories cannot begin to explain how God will clothe His people with light, yet God has a plan to do it. It will be beautiful beyond description. Light and color will shine forth out of our beings.

> "Come, I will show you the bride, the Lamb's wife." He...showed me the great city, the holy Jerusalem, descending out of heaven from God, having the glory of God. Her light was like a most precious stone, like a jasper stone, clear as crystal. (Revelation 21:9-11)

> "Many of those who sleep in the dust of the earth shall awake, some to everlasting life...Those who are wise shall shine like the brightness of the firmament...like the stars forever and ever." (Daniel 12:2-3)

> "The righteous will shine forth as the sun in the kingdom of their Father." (Matthew 13:43)

Our future bodies will be filled with God's power and glory. While our physical bodies are sown in dishonor and addiction to sin, sometimes racked with sickness, they will be raised in the glory of God. Our bodies are sown in corruption—meaning they rot in the grave—but they will be raised in incorruption.

> There is one glory of the sun, another glory of the moon, and another glory of the stars; for one star differs from another star in glory. So also is the resurrection of the dead. The body is sown in corruption, it is raised in incorruption. It is sown in dishonor, it is raised in glory. It is sown in weakness, it is

raised in power. It is sown a natural body, it is raised
a spiritual body. (1 Corinthians 15:41-44)

The apostle Paul wrote that we will experience what it
means to be clothed in light and to possess incredible power in
our resurrected bodies. This body will be much more powerful
and beautiful than the one in which we currently live. We literally cannot imagine what this will be like, because everything
we know in the physical dimension is in relation to how extremely limiting it is. We judge how far we can jump before we
fall. We judge how fast we can run based on how much faster
someone else ran the same distance. All we can comprehend is
based on what we're not able to do. God says, "On that day, I
will give you a form you have no grid for. I am taking the limits
off this new design."

Our culture has made the afterlife seem to be some sort
of cloud-based harp recital, where the seraphim wander from
cloud to cloud, giving tips on playing lullabies while cherubs
float to and fro with snack trays. Compared to what God
really has planned for us in the next age, this idea is boring!
Who wants to play a harp for the next million years? We are
being groomed to rule and reign alongside the King, and we
will do it in new bodies that are indescribably beautiful. Our
glorified bodies will have supernatural abilities in relation to
communication, strength, senses, and a myriad of other areas.
We might be able to communicate in many languages. Our
communication through music and poetic expression will be
absolutely beautiful. You will pick the instruments you've always
wanted to play to express God's beauty and you'll be able to play
them with excellence.

Our resurrected bodies will have the supernatural beauty,
properties, and abilities that Jesus' body has. We will have supernatural abilities in our five senses. We will all have excellent
sight at a distance as well as at close range. We will be able
to hear at distances, with great perception and perfect balance.
Our taste buds will enjoy food beyond anything we can cur-

rently imagine. One reason God determined to have food in the age to come is simply so that we might enjoy it. God will be glorified as we enjoy eating in eternity.

> Whether you eat or drink...do all to the glory of
> God. (1 Corinthians 10:31)

Our sense of touch will give us the ability to feel perfectly and to discern objects with great clarity. Our sense of smell will give us the ability to enjoy and discern what is going on in the environment around us. The speed and endurance of our physical bodies will be supernatural. We will be able to work and play for long hours without feeling drained. There will be no fatigue, no sickness, no death. We will have perfect energy at all times. Philip's translation from one location to another is probably the best example of what it will be like.

> Now when they came up out of the water, the Spirit
> of the Lord caught Philip away, so that the eunuch
> saw him no more...Philip was found at Azotus.
> (Acts 8:39-40)

God is not merely interested in beautifying individuals; He is preparing to beautify His Bride as a whole. The Father is committed to making a beautiful Bride for His beautiful Son.

> Then I, John, saw the holy city, New Jerusalem,
> coming down out of heaven from God, prepared as
> a bride adorned for her husband. (Revelation 21:2)

On that day, as the New Jerusalem descends, its beauty will be unlike anything seen on the earth. What strange phrasing, comparing a city to a bride. John spoke about some of the beauty of the New Jerusalem being due to its citizens. The eternal city is called the Bride because of the inhabitants who govern it. The glory of the city lies in the residents of the city. The current cities of the earth are known by the characteristics of their citizens. Even though the cities themselves are only made of buildings and streets and trees, one city is said to be friendly while another is said to be hostile. The city's reputation is based on the characteristics of the people who live there. A city considered generous is only described in such a way because it is filled with generous people. The New Jerusalem will be glorious and beautiful because of the nature of her glorious and beautiful citizens. The Bride of Christ, the most glorious and beautiful of all created beings, will radiate her glory as she governs that city.

Being called a beautiful bride has far-reaching ramifications. A bride is not a buddy or even a girlfriend. A bride walks in a newly-acquired level of ownership in relation to everything her bridegroom possesses. Time and time again the Word of God tells us we actually become partakers of God's glory. Jesus said, "The glory which You gave Me I have given them" (John 17:22). Jesus longed to impart His glory and beauty to us. The writer of Hebrews makes mention of it as well. We will be crowned with God's glory and beauty. "...You have crowned him [the redeemed] with glory and honor..." (Hebrews 2:7, 10).

As the Bride of Christ comes to her senses, she will respond like the prodigal son as he realized how far he was from home. She will be shocked and wonder, "Will He accept me?" In her moment of weakness, God will come alongside her, and, by virtue of His desire for her, make her valuable. Desire brings worth, remember? Every bit of her beauty is a reflection of His.

BEAUTY PREPARATION

Not only does Scripture point to a day when we will be fully what God intends, it also tells us that the very trials we face today help to make this glory a reality in our lives. Today's troubles are a school of sorts—a university of beauty—preparing us for life in eternity with Him. The sooner we realize the divine purpose of this beautification process, this preparation, the sooner we begin to give ourselves to it, painful as it may be.

> For our light affliction, which is but for a moment,
> is working for us a far more exceeding and eternal
> weight of glory... (2 Corinthians 4:17)

In the book of Esther, God reveals His purpose to beautify His people. Esther goes through beauty preparations in order to be made ready for the king, which is a prophetic picture of the Bride of Christ preparing for her King. We go through the necessary beauty preparations in this age so we will be counted worthy of the Son when He returns to set up His kingdom on the earth.

It is not always easy to see how troubles and struggles can pave the way for beauty; once in a while there is a glimpse in one person's life that serves as a beacon to the rest of us. Dennis Byrd is one of those individuals. On November 29, 1992, the New York Jets lined up against the Kansas City Chiefs. Dennis was a broad-shouldered and blonde-haired defensive tackle at the peak of his athletic career. But that day he had a jarring, head-on collision with a teammate. An unexpected shock went through Dennis' entire body and he lay suddenly limp on the field. He was permanently paralyzed from the neck down.

He went through countless surgeries and treatments with little progress. Months later he lay in the hospital bed of a rehabilitation facility as a reporter interviewed him for a primetime special. After telling the story of Dennis' career with interviews and video clips, the reporter commented that the football player must have a very strong faith. Dennis said quietly, "Yes, I am a believer in Jesus Christ." When the reporter asked how Dennis' faith could be reconciled with having endured such a horrible accident, he probably wasn't expecting the answer he received. With the conviction of a man who had thought this through a thousand times, Dennis leveled his steely gaze at the camera and said, "For I consider that the sufferings of this present time are not worthy to be compared with the glory that shall be revealed in us" (Romans 8:18).

In that moment, Dennis exhibited a profound understanding of God that many people in less drastic circumstances are unable to grasp: even our trials and afflictions can change us forever for the better. It's not that God wants to see us broken, but rather He wants us to see our own brokenness. Dennis was not minimizing his misfortune. He was placing it in the context of eternity. He knew this was not the first time God had overlooked his broken humanity. In his physical and emotional brokenness, Dennis was being beautified. The same is true for every one of us who walks in relationship with Jesus—He is committed to giving us beauty for ashes. The beauty available to us in God is not merely something we observe from afar or hope to attain in some distant future. It is, in fact, highly practical. God tells us in His Word that His very beauty or glory can be placed within us. While the pagan religions of that era built temples and shrines to hold their concept of the presence of a god, the writer of Ephesians said humanity itself was made for the very indwelling of God.

> ...you are...built together for a dwelling place of
> God in the Spirit. (Ephesians 2:22)

This indwelling of God is how God, the consuming fire, chooses to express His glory, His grandeur, His love, and His beauty to the rest of creation for all time. It is a mystery of cosmic proportions that the holy God would not only fashion a Bride for Himself out of the dust of the earth, but that He would go on to dwell *within* her, giving her a measure of beauty worthy of His infinite affection.

BEAUTIFIED HEARTS AND MINDS

Even more remarkable than God dwelling in the hearts of men and women, expressing His divine beauty through them, is God going further and depositing His life into them as well. It is mind-blowing to think that He would show us His beauty on the inside; but to go so far as to put His life in us and enable us to show His life to others is even more profound. This holy indwelling that brings us into our place as a beautiful Bride has a distinct effect on our hearts and minds. God dwelling in us affects how we think, speak, and feel.

"This is the covenant that I will make them...I will
put my laws into their hearts, and in their minds I
will write them..." (Hebrews 10:16)

In the process of beautifying His Bride, Jesus writes the
laws of His Father on her mind and heart. She will understand
God with her mind and feel Him with her heart. Supernatural thoughts will come to us forever. As we rule with Christ,
partially in this age and in fullness in the age to come, we will
enter into a realm of understanding that surpasses the great
and learned men and women of history. We have been given
access to the very thoughts and thought processes of God (1
Corinthians 2:16). The concept that He writes on our minds
and hearts speaks of His supernatural enlargement of our capacity for understanding and love. He will crown us with radiant
and beautiful minds and hearts; just like Jesus, we will be filled
with divine intelligence and hearts overflowing with love. In the
age to come there will still be mathematics, science, technology, food, art, and music. These disciplines will not suddenly
disappear. We will have great intelligence that will enhance our
communication with Jesus, our Bridegroom God. We will also
have supernatural abilities to communicate with perfect speech,
musical ability, singing ability, thought, and expression.

Our minds and hearts will be expanded with new capacity
for holiness, and with holiness, a deeper sense of satisfaction.
This will beautify us. Along with supernatural understanding of
truth, Jesus will give us supernatural ability to feel things like He
does. Our hearts will be beautified as we experience the same
feelings and emotions as Jesus. We will have the capacity to love
more as we are empowered with holy affections for God and
others. The love of God will be poured out in our hearts by the
Holy Spirit (Romans 5:5). The very love with which the Father
loved Jesus will be in us (John 17:26). We will love to a degree
that goes far beyond anything we can presently imagine.

With this love and with our increased emotional capacities,
we will have no envy and no jealousy. We will not compare

ourselves with others and we will not bring accusations against ourselves or anyone else. We will be devoid of all condemnation, fear of failure, competition, discouragement, addiction, and negative feelings. These things will have been replaced by massive capacities for happiness and contentment, peace and joy, unity, and love, as evidenced by having joy *inexpressible* and *fullness* of glory.

> Yet believing, you rejoice with joy inexpressible and full of glory. (1 Peter 1:8)

Jesus will not rule with a depressed Bride. We must understand what Jesus is thinking, and feel what He is feeling. We will be unified with the flow of His heart forever. One day soon we will know a supernatural unity in relationship like that which currently only exists within the Godhead. Jesus' prayer in John 17:12, "That they all may be one, as You, Father, are in Me, and I in You; that they also may be one in Us…" will be answered.

The John 17:12 passage is often used to promote unity among city leaders, and there are certainly facets of that reflected in Jesus' words. However the goal He set—unity among humans reflecting the unity of the Trinity—is so lofty it can only be perfectly achieved among beings who have been made like Him. The only people who can find unity like that will have to be completely convinced that Jesus sees them as beautiful and, in understanding their own beauty, be willing to run the risk of wholly loving another person because Jesus thinks that other person is beautiful too.

CHAPTER FOUR

The Longing for Greatness

This game has a hundred variations and is probably played by children in every people group on the face of the earth. In the American Midwest a bale of hay is used. In Siberia, it's a pile of snow at the end of a freshly plowed street. Everywhere children gather and human instincts prevail, the game is played. It is known by many names, but where I grew up, we called it "king of the hill." It can be played by individuals or highly organized teams, although to be truthful, even the best team leader can fall victim to a mutiny by the time it's over. The desire to be the last man standing, the de facto king of the hill, proves too tempting to resist. Eventually, the strongest alliances fail and it's every man for himself.

The game starts in childhood, but most people play it for the rest of their lives. Perhaps not in the all-out way of pushing people around, the echoes of dog-eat-dog and at-any-cost mentalities prevail. The king of the hill becomes king of the boardroom, king of academia, king of the home, or even king of the pulpit committee. There is something within the heart of man that yearns to be crowned with greatness. Whether wrangling for control of a dirt hill on the edge of a playground or control of a group of people we're called to serve, we're usually driven by similar motives. We want to be great. This desire has taken a lot of hard knocks over the years. Striving for greatness has driven a lot of people to do ungodly things as they try to fulfill their desire at any cost. As a result, adult etiquette seems to shun any desire for greatness, to stuff it down somewhere in our psyche and feign humility, all the while smoldering on the inside because someone else gets recognized and we get ignored.

I want to challenge you to think about greatness in another way. What if you were destined for greatness? I'm not talking about being arrogant or putting others down in order to be seen as the best. I'm asking, what if part of God's plan was to make you truly great for eternity? Would you have to go about pursuing it like we did as kids, knocking people off the hill on your way to the top? Or would God have some counter-culture way for us to achieve exactly what He has for us?

Allow me to let you in on a little-known secret. You desire to be great precisely because you were meant to be great. That doesn't negate the wrongs associated with striving for worldly honor and acclaim with a spirit of pride. It's still wrong to knock one another off the top of the hill, it's still wrong to backstab in the boardroom, and it's still wrong to bully the pulpit committee just so you can achieve your advancement. True to His style and reputation, God has a much more excellent plan to fulfill your longing for greatness. The great God built into your spirit a longing to be great and successful. Greatness is part of your divine calling. Jesus never rebuked anyone for longing to be great, only for attempting to fulfill the longing in a wrong way (Luke 11:43). We are not to repent of this God-given longing to be great. We are only to repent of pursuing it with a wrong spirit.

We were made for greatness and honor. Every believer is ordained for greatness beyond anything we can fathom. Paul described the greatness God has planned for us as something that has not even entered the human mind when he wrote, "Eye has not seen, nor ear heard, nor have entered into the heart of man the things which God has prepared for those who love Him" (1 Corinthians 2:9).

Let me tell you, I unashamedly want to be great in God's sight! I want to be wealthy eternally! I encourage all godly people to have this as a personal goal. Greatness is within the reach of everyone. Get rid of your false humility, but remember that the only way into greatness is through the cross of Jesus and by walking in meekness.

JESUS MADE A PROMISE

The book of Revelation was written sixty years after Jesus ascended in the resurrection to be with His Father in heaven. Certainly, during those sixty years, small groups of believers sat around the fire wondering, "If He were to appear tonight, what would He say?" Sitting on the island of Patmos, John found out. Sixty years after His ascension, Jesus gave encouragement and correction to seven churches in Asia Minor (Revelation 2–3). To the Laodicean church, Jesus gave a staggering promise of greatness. He said, "To him who overcomes I will grant to sit with Me on My throne" (Revelation 3:21). This is one of the most amazing statements in Scripture. Nobody sits in God's presence. Every creature described is pictured as standing in respect or prostrate in holy adoration when appearing before God. Yet in this passage we read of saints sitting in God's presence. This is one of the most stunning statements I can imagine. Do we have any idea who we are?

God satisfies our longing to be great by granting us, His Bride, a position of authority surpassing even the highest-ranking angels. The revelation of the redeemed as enthroned with Jesus answers our cry to be successful. The promise that Jesus' disciples will sit with Him on His own throne must have been so strange to John. Just think about it. Here in the United States we have a certain protocol. There are certain things that are simply not done. When you go to the White House, even as an invited guest, you do not sit behind the desk in the Oval Office and put your feet up. To do so would be the ultimate in presumption—that desk belongs to someone else. While stealing someone's pew in church on Sunday is forgivable, you certainly wouldn't take the President's seat in his own office.

Take that absurd example, multiply it a billion times, and you still have not begun to approach what it would be like to sit with Jesus on His throne. When John received this from the Lord, he probably pondered a while. *Sit on His throne? What does He mean?* It means we will rule and reign with Him. We will help rule over a vast eternal empire called the kingdom of God. We will be entrusted with the most significant tasks in ruling this eternal city. This means the Church is at the pinnacle of power in the created order. Nothing could ever compare to the greatness of the Bride of Christ when she takes her seat next to her Bridegroom. In offering her His chair, He says, "You were made for this; you were destined for greatness."

As John reflected on this, he probably remembered other things Jesus said during His three-year public ministry. I can imagine John smiling and thinking, "Sixty years later and I'm still piecing all this together!" John might have thought about Jesus teaching on a hillside one day. Jesus had said many profound things that afternoon, but two phrases suddenly stuck out.

> "Rejoice and be exceedingly glad, for great is your reward in heaven..." (Matthew 5:12)

> "...whoever does and teaches them [God's commandments], he shall be called great in the kingdom of heaven." (Matthew 5:19)

Even then, Jesus was laying the groundwork for this understanding. We were destined for greatness and it is within our grasp if we choose it. The longing to be great, to be noble and to be successful is answered by God when He enthrones us as His bridal partner in eternity. As the Bride of Christ, we are given the highest position of honor and authority in the eternal city. Romans 8:17 tells us we will be coheirs with Jesus. This is an expression of how He feels about us.

Every social order has a ruling class. Generally, it's a small number of the population. This aristocracy controls the finances, the power and even the land in most instances. There aren't too many opportunities to break into this aristocracy. One usually has to be born into it. The other way to become a part of the ruling class is to marry into the aristocracy. Well, as a believer, you have married into money and power in a big way, an extreme way. In becoming the Bride of Christ, you have married into indescribable power. You are part of the aristocracy in the eternal city, part of the ruling upper class of God's eternal empire. You are royalty. This is not to say the redeemed will be equal to God. That is a lie Satan has successfully used in many false religions. But you *will* reign on the earth as a king and priest.

> "[Jesus] made us kings and priests to our God...we shall reign on the earth." (Revelation 5:10)

All of this seems too heady to truthfully consider. Jesus wants us to be great? To be kings and priests? As kings, the saints will reign with judicial responsibility and authority on the earth in the age to come. Knowing our own hearts, we wonder how this can be. We have not progressed far past our childhood "king of the hill" days. It's hard to believe Jesus would choose to present us to His Father as coheirs of the kingdom. There seems to be a lot of work to do before we're ready for that role. Fortunately, Jesus always makes a way. He never appoints us to anything without providing a process of preparation. Esther, the young Jewish girl who found herself in the court of royalty, had her time of preparation before she approached the king (Esther 2). Timothy had his apprenticeship with Paul before being launched into ministry. The primary preparation on the pathway to greatness is entirely different from what we would do by nature.

> "Whoever desires to become great among you, let him be your servant. And whoever desires to be first among you, let him be your slave." (Matthew 20:26-27)

> "Whoever humbles himself...is the greatest in the

kingdom of heaven." (Matthew 18:4)

Although the picture of servants and slaves bears little resemblance to today's Western culture, the concept is still sound. Servants attend to every whim of the master and, if they are faithful in their roles, they'll still be servants at the end of their days. Jesus turned this concept upside down, saying that making oneself a servant is the only route to true greatness. We have a fundamental misunderstanding about our roles here on earth. There is a great drive to be all we can be now. This is driven by the idea that we get one chance at life and if we don't maximize every opportunity we will miss out. We seek the highest station in life we can achieve, somehow believing it will be used for the ultimate good, and this is the motive that drives us. Many times we couldn't be more wrong.

Jesus was approached by a rich man who wanted to know more about following Him (Matthew 19:16-30). Somehow, this rich young man instinctively knew that the life he was living was not going to fit the bill. He had achieved greatness in the eyes of his peers and still knew, from the perspective of heaven, he was lacking. The young man knew about more than just money; he also knew Jewish law. An apostate, cheating, two-dimensional villain he was *not*. When Jesus told him some of the commandments, the rich young ruler assured Him that he had lived them out faithfully, but was still convinced he lacked something.

He was right. Jesus told him if he wanted to be perfect, he should sell his possessions and give the money to the poor; that way he would have treasure in heaven. Jesus then told him to follow Him. In saying this, Jesus was not orchestrating a fundraiser. He was making a point to the man and the disciples: the point that money and position make it more difficult to make the necessary life adjustments to pursue God wholeheartedly. The Bible says the man walked away in sadness because he had great wealth. Jesus chose this moment to drive home a point to his followers:

> Then Jesus said to His disciples, "Assuredly, I say to
> you that it is hard for a rich man to enter the king-
> dom of heaven." (Matthew 19:23)

Jesus was not condemning wealth or social position. He was illustrating the point that this man had so much emotionally invested in his assignment in this life that he was unable to consider letting go of any of it in order to pursue his assignment in the next age. The young man had people reporting to him, status, and responsibility. In his mind, he had achieved greatness—a greatness difficult to let go of even to the smallest degree. Today we constantly live in the tension of weighing our assignment in this life against our long-term assignment in the age to come. Rest assured, whatever you're doing right now, you probably won't be doing it during the millennial reign or the eternal age!

At the International House of Prayer, we run five different internships. At any given moment, there are at least 300 people of all ages, married and single, who are serving as short-term interns here. College students take a semester off from their studies to pursue the Lord full-time; retired people invest what some people would consider their leisure years in the prayer room; married couples uproot their families and move across the country to raise their children in the environment of 24/7 prayer; there's even a nocturnal group we call "Fire in the Night," comprised of people who minister before the Lord through the night hours. The lives of all these people are structured around the prayer room, classes, and serving the missions base ministries.

Very few of our interns find themselves on the platform during these internships. They will rarely sing during a conference or speak to a large group. They're aware of this before they start the program. These interns come to serve and learn for a few months. They understand that the purpose of an internship is to learn the basics of how we do things and to allow God to form their hearts. What is interesting is that after a period of serving, a high percentage of them stay on as full-time staff members and eventually find themselves in leadership roles, based largely on the servanthood they exhibited during their internships. Choosing the low road makes a way for them later.

I view our life in this age as a seventy-year internship (Psalm 90:10) that prepares us for our life on earth in the age to come. Our next stage of life in the age to come starts in the millennial kingdom. This is our primary ministry assignment and it lasts for one thousand years (Revelation 20:4-6; 2:26-27; 3:21; 5:10; 22:5). In this "seventy-year internship" we determine to what degree we want to function in His government in the age to come. The measure to which we develop in love, meekness, and revelation during our lives now determines our positions and functions in His government (Matthew 7:14; 19:30; 20:16, 26-27; 22:14; Luke 13:24). Our ministries in the age to come have nothing to do with how much we accomplished outwardly in this age, but rather how much we developed inwardly. The choices we make in our seventy-year internship determine where and how we will function in our next assignment. There exists a dynamic continuity between our lives now and what happens to us in the next age.

Like the rich young ruler, most people fail to understand this. They fall for the idea that they must live out their longing for greatness during life in this age, so they push, prod and poke their way to the top of the hill. Obviously, most never make it. A few become great in the earthly sense, but only until someone younger or stronger knocks them off their dirt-clod throne. Worse yet, they reach the end of their lives and find that they have wasted their earthly lives, pursuing greatness in the eyes of others at the expense of greatness in the age to come.

I unashamedly want to be great, but not just for seventy years on earth. In fact, I am willing to forgo greatness or human acclaim on this side of glory in order to be all I can be in the next age. I would gladly trade the temporal recognition of my peers for the eternal recognition of my King. I am no different from the rest of the world in my longing to be great. I'm just determined to focus on seeking it in a different time frame.

So then what determines a successful seventy-year intern-ship? What sorts of things will ensure that we fulfill our longing for greatness in the realm where it really matters and really lasts? No matter how big or glorious, our ministry or marketplace as-signment is only our first assignment; it remains a temporary assignment. We get our next assignment based not on how big our first assignment was, but on how much meekness we devel-oped in it. The majority of people are putting all their eggs in the wrong basket. They put all of their energy into making their first assignment big in the eyes of others, or successful by the reckoning of their peers and associates. Jesus said that it is hard for the rich to be great. Why? Because they are so distracted by their riches in their first assignment. They become so captured by their temporal power and greatness that they cannot em-brace a lifestyle assuring them greatness in the age to come. It is hard because their first assignment consumes them and they lose sight of their next, eternal assignment.

God has given us the gift of greatness that lasts forever. It has nothing to do with how big our ministries are, how big our bank accounts are, how many people like us, or how many people get healed when we pray for them. It is something that transcends all of those realities.

UNDERSTANDING OUR INHERITANCE WITH GOD

The Father has planned a dynamic inheritance for Jesus, to give Him an eternal companion, the Bride of Christ. As believers re-ceive the truth of who they really are as Jesus' inheritance, their lives will portray a divine inner strength and a fierce determina-tion to be wholly His. Paul prayed that we would understand the riches of the glory of being Jesus' inheritance.

> ...the Father of glory, may give to you the spirit of
> wisdom and revelation in the knowledge of Him,
> the eyes of your understanding being enlightened;
> that you may know...what are the riches of the glo-

ry of [Jesus'] inheritance in the saints... (Ephesians
1:17-18)

We need the eyes of our hearts opened so that we can know
what are the riches of the glory of being God's inheritance.
There is a wealth of glory you and I possess because we are the
objects of His desire. We are His inheritance; we are the ones
the Father chose for Jesus. Jesus wants us to be His and to reign
with Him. When this touches our hearts by revelation, we enter
into what is called the riches of God's glory, or the depth of the
vast wealth of this reality. Beloved, by the sheer virtue of this
we are very successful in God. When we understand that we
are Jesus' inheritance, we begin to appreciate that vast wealth
belongs to us—a wealth that can never be taken from us. It is
secure forever.

When our hearts connect with the profound greatness
we already possess, it changes our emotional chemistry. We
feel much stronger on the inside as we gain confidence in our
greatness and value before God. We see that our greatness is not
based on what we look like physically, on how big our ministry
is, or how much money we have. We gain an unwavering
stability in our inner man because we understand our profound
greatness before God. Thus, small ministries in this age do not
need to offend us. Waiting cannot offend us. We are anchored in
another reality—in the riches of the glory of who we are as His
inheritance (Ephesians 1:18).

As the Church takes hold of the truth of who we really are
as honored and esteemed heirs of God's throne, our lives will
portray a divine inner strength and a fierce determination to
give ourselves completely to Him. In Jesus, you married into
indescribable wealth and power. Kings do not walk as beggars,
because they have plenty in their storehouses and treasuries.
They do not worry about receiving the praise of others, because
they have confidence in their place of power in their empires.
The amount of emotional energy we expend trying to establish
our own sense of success and importance is massive. The gift of

greatness has been given to us wrapped in the revelation of the Bridegroom God, Christ Jesus.

WILLINGNESS

Most people at one time or another entertain a dream of finding their way into a role where they wield great power, work short hours, and have time enough to pursue recreation, paid for, of course, by a comfortable salary. Somewhere along the line, these people graduate and enter the real world, where they receive a rude awakening. The "executive position" with their uncle's company turned out to be in the mail room. That sales position proved to be all commission, which quickly translated into no commission. Expecting to land on top of the hill, they found themselves at the bottom staring up, and no one was willing to team up with them to get to the top. In that place of disappointment, they enter a testing period. In lieu of the perfect opportunity, what will they do? Will they ignore lesser opportunities at hand and hope to land the big job? Or will they roll up their sleeves and get down to business?

With a mindset that this life is all there is, it might make sense to wait for a better job while you still have the chance, even though good jobs rarely fall out of the sky. However, if you look at this earthly life as an internship for the next, you realize that those lowly roles we so often end up with are actually valuable training for our hearts and our heads. The skills with which we master the low wire will serve us greatly when it's our turn on the high wire. In fact, thinking of it that way, why do we really want to start on the high wire anyway?

One of our ministry leaders worked his way through Bible college. Completely convinced that all his fellow students were out planting churches that would grow to a thousand members by the time fall arrived and they had to return to school, he took the only summer job he could find. It was at the last full-service gas station in town. Not only was he pumping gas while his friends preached the gospel, he was the only one in town doing so!

Looking back on that job, he'll tell you it actually was quite beneficial for ministry. Almost everyone buys gasoline. In watching the stream of customers come through the gas station that summer, he learned more about human nature than he did in his college psychology classes. He tried to give everyone the same service, occasionally surprising the poor fellow driving a beaten up old station wagon by insisting on washing the windshield just as if it were a sports car. He learned about doing the job that you have until the job you want comes along. In short, he learned about doing little things well.

Scripture tells us of a time when Jesus spoke to a group of people who anticipated that He was going to overthrow the governments of Rome and Israel. They expected him to bring His kingdom in very quickly, and they wanted to be lined up for positions of influence when He did. They were the first-century equivalent of the college student dreaming about his perfect first job. Sensing that He needed to stress the secondary nature of this life and the reality of a coming kingdom that awarded greatness on a very different scale, Jesus told the story of a demanding man who gave his servants varying levels of responsibility. He illustrated the principle of being willing to work hard at the beginner level when the man in the story told his employee, "Well done...because you were faithful in a very little, have authority over ten cities" (Luke 19:17).

Jesus showed that doing little things well right now leads to opportunities for doing big things later. While that is true in the natural, it is doubly true in the spiritual realm. Being a willing and humble worker in this age translates directly into having authority in the age to come. It's counterintuitive to our impatient and incomplete ideas of greatness, but time and again we see it played out in Jesus' teaching.

FAITHFULNESS

One of the most important factors involved in determining

greatness in the age to come is that of faithfulness. The old adage says that the road to hell is paved with good intentions. While that is true, it is equally true that there's a side road made of the same stuff: it leads absolutely nowhere. Ask any leader how many volunteers they've had to track down due to neglected commitments. Sunday school teachers don't show up. Communion trays don't get filled. Trash does not get taken out. These are the minor infractions! On the other end of the spectrum, employees betray their bosses and married couples are unfaithful to one another.

People often ask us what it was like to start the house of prayer. I reply, "Little, rough, and ugly!" Worship leaders doubled as the cleaning crew, prayer leaders doubled as sound techs, and sound techs doubled as ushers. In the hectic time that offered so many jobs to so few workers, I was approached by one of our worship leaders who said, "What can I do to help? I'll do anything." I wish I could say I prayed about it; that would make the whole story sound more spiritual! Instead, I just saw a need and put someone to work: "Would you manage the cleaning of the building for us?" It should be pointed out that "the building" was a sorry ensemble of three old office trailers huddled together on a parking lot with craters you could lose a car in. We had a couple of meeting rooms and four bathrooms. "Managing cleaning" was more cleaning than managing. Gregg, the worship leader in question, found himself cleaning toilets and picking up trash. He distinguished himself with his smile. He was serving in a low position, but doing it with joy.

Fast-forward seven years. The International House of Prayer had grown from a handful of interns to 400 staff members and 300 interns, as well as another 300 Bible school students. Gregg was still leading worship. By this time he'd recorded a couple of CDs and was doing some international traveling. But here's the amazing part: he was still cleaning our restrooms. Our facilities had grown to include multiple buildings on four different sites. Even though he now had a crew of interns and others to assist him, he was still essentially doing the job I'd asked him to do seven years before. In between scheduling workers and ordering soap, he could still be found unclogging a toilet. And in seven years, his smile never wavered. It was simply amazing!

After serving for seven years, he announced that he and his wife were going to be doing more international travel. Their giftings had opened doors for them in Europe, meaning they would be gone for two or three months at a time. With regret, he handed back the role he'd volunteered for seven years earlier. I think Gregg is the kind of person Jesus was speaking of in Matthew 25, when He told the story about people's differing reactions to responsibility. He described a master who left his workers in charge of a variety of things, only to return after a long time to see how they were doing. When finding a servant who had done exceptionally well, the master said: "Well done, good and faithful servant; you were faithful over a *few things*, I will make you ruler over *many things*. Enter into the joy of your lord" (Matthew 25:21).

The day Gregg handed his duties over to his replacement, we had him come up on the platform during a staff meeting. The room erupted with spontaneous applause in appreciation of his service. I enjoyed telling the story to the new staff members of how he had volunteered for what we both assumed would be just a few months, and how he had served faithfully in that role for seven years. The staff cheered him with such gusto because they recognized this was a great man in the kingdom.

RESISTING SELF-PROMOTION

Self-promotion is such a part of the human experience that we have a difficult time detecting it in our own lives. For many of us, it is as natural as breathing. One of the grand traditions of elementary education is the "line leader." Most classrooms have some form of this exercise. Children are chosen to be the day's line leader, perhaps by a prescribed pattern or perhaps at random. Whatever the method by which they land their role, it is a role they relish. They lead the class in the Pledge of Allegiance, on the walk to the lunchroom, out to recess, and then to the bus waiting area at the end of the day. To their fellow first-graders, they are special for the day. Sometimes they are honored with a hat or a tiara. Make no mistake about it: this is their day. Heaven help the poor child who falls ill and misses his or her chance to be line leader. The very children who would have cheered them on in their capacity as line leader suddenly begin to jockey for the role.

From first grade to the nursing home, not much changes in human behavior. There are always plenty of people wanting to be line leader at age seven and age seventy and every age in between. On the surface, they might express joy when you're the line leader, but if you happen to fall sick at lunchtime, theirs will be the first hand raised in hopes of taking the job. None of this is new. Only a few verses after talking with the rich young ruler, Jesus found himself in a discussion with Simon Peter, who was quick to draw a distinction between himself and the rich young ruler. "Jesus," Simon said, "we have left everything to follow you." He then got to his real point: "What then will there be for us?" Even in expressing his willingness to leave his fishing business behind him, Simon was maneuvering for position: "Remember, Jesus, we gave it all up—so when is pay day?"

I think there was probably a smile on Jesus' face when He answered. Not because of Peter's failings—Jesus knew he would ultimately be a resounding success in ministry—but because Jesus also knew everything Peter would have to go through before he really comprehended the lesson he was about to hear.

> "But many who are first will be last, and *the last first.*"
> (Matthew 19:30)

I suspect the disciples all nodded thoughtfully until the moment Jesus turned His back, when they began to compare notes. "What did He say? The first becomes last? The last, first? What is He talking about? He's got this whole leadership structure upside down!"

They were right about that. Jesus did turn the structure for leadership—indeed, the entire path to greatness—completely upside down with that statement. For centuries, people had operated in the opposite spirit of this teaching, and for centuries to come they would continue to do so. They would usurp the authority they thought was owed them. They would rush to put themselves in places of leadership rather than wait to be placed there. Just to drive home the point, Jesus reiterated it in the very next chapter.

> "The last will be first, and the first last. For many are called, but few chosen." (Matthew 20:16)

The call to greatness is issued to every human being. It is in the potential destiny of each individual to reign with Christ. Jesus knew, however, that many people would not resist the temptation to self-promotion, and by putting themselves in first place during their seventy-year internships, would find themselves in last place for eternity. As noted, it all comes back to the idea of servanthood prescribed in Matthew 20:26, where Jesus said, "Whoever desires to become great among you, let him be your servant."

We fail to understand this simple teaching when we make a false assumption that what exists on earth prior to the second coming of Christ is automatically irrelevant and disregarded in the Millennium, as if Jesus has no interest in the posture of our hearts today. While these are two distinct periods of time with unique characteristics and parameters, there exists a dynamic continuity between our behavior in this present life and our roles in the age to come. Our attitudes, our deeds, our characters, and much more that we have developed in this age will be carried over to the next.

The thief on the cross who begged for forgiveness in the last moments of his life must have been shocked when he stepped over the line into paradise after Jesus told him he would (Luke 23:43). I imagine this former thief walking the streets of gold, shocked at the robe he was given and the greetings he received from the angels. When he asked what it was all about, one of the angels told him, "You don't understand—you're a king here." The thief looked at the angel, stunned. "A king?" he asked. "If I had known I was a king, I would have never lived as a thief!"

Many people live like thieves, stealing honor and garnering greatness where it is not deserved, unaware that their destinies are greatness. Today, do your best to live as one destined to be a king in the age to come by exhibiting humility to all people in all situations. Greatness is your destiny. It is God's gift to you.

CHAPTER FIVE

The Longing for Intimacy without Shame

Before the beginning of time, the Father burned with the desire to have a family, to know them and be known by them in a deep and profound way. That is why He fashioned the human heart to long for intimacy with Him and with others. God's dream has always been to share His heart with us in a way far surpassing anything we know or can imagine now. God created us with a profound desire to fully know and to be fully known without shame. Consider that the One who created everything knows every movement of our hearts, and He wants to share His heart with us. Our value to Him compels Him to invite us into this mysterious realm of nearness to Him. God satisfies this longing by revealing His heart to us and by communicating how much He truly does know us. We only enjoy a down payment of this reality in the current age, but we'll experience the fullness of it in the age to come.

> For now we see in a mirror, dimly, but then face to face. Now I know in part, but then I shall know just as I also am known. (1 Corinthians 13:12)

This mutual sharing is an expression of God's affection for us. Without this, our lives would be exceedingly lonely. Henry David Thoreau said, "The mass of men lead lives of quiet desperation." Most people live with a devastating sense of loneliness in this life. Tragically, they live without sharing their joys and sorrows with anyone. We were created in such a way that loneliness severely breaks and bruises us. This is not God's plan for us. Rather, God's people are meant to have intimacy and unity with each other, because the Father has permitted Jesus to pour His glory out on us now in part, and in fullness in the age to come.

> "That they all may be one, as You, Father, are in Me, and I in You; that they also may be one in Us...the glory which You gave Me I have given them, that they may be one just as We are one...that they may be made perfect in one..." (John 17:21-23)

Because of Jesus, we need not fear being left to experience the mysteries and the ups and downs of life alone. This longing for companionship will be answered partially in this age and fully in the age to come. The Father is the one who first observed that loneliness is not good for the human spirit, remarking in Genesis 2:18 how "it is not good that man should be alone." This truth was not communicated as a criticism of solitude in seeking after God in private, but regarding loneliness. There is a huge difference. The human heart craves intimacy; therefore, the enemy seeks to exploit this by bringing us down many avenues that offer a counterfeit intimacy which in turn brings shame. The irony is that when we accept what the enemy offers, we minimize our chances of experiencing real intimacy, leaving ourselves open to loneliness even in the midst of multitudes. In loneliness, Satan can destroy people much more easily.

Think of the person you respect most in life. Imagine the joy of knowing they desired you and trusted you enough to reveal their deepest secrets to you. Well, God trusts us with the deep things of His heart. It seems unimaginable that such a great God longs to be intimately connected to broken people. It is really an indescribable privilege.

More than 2,500 years after Adam and Eve were first in the garden of Eden, Moses wrote their story in the early chapters of

Genesis. Moses pointed to the glory of married love when he described how God brought Adam and Eve together to become one flesh. He emphasized that they were naked and experienced no shame.

> Therefore a man shall leave his father and mother and be joined to his wife, and they shall become one flesh. And they were both naked, the man and his wife, and were not ashamed. (Genesis 2:24-25)

Another 1,500 years after Moses wrote this, the apostle Paul gave additional insight into Moses' account. Paul knew something about God's heart that Moses did not know. Paul quoted Genesis 2:18 in Ephesians 5:31-32, applying it to the spiritual relationship between Jesus and the Church. The creation of Adam and Eve to become one flesh is a prophetic picture of the way that Jesus will be joined to His church. Paul referred to this as God's great mystery. Spiritually speaking, being naked and unashamed means all the secrets of our hearts will be fully unveiled. We will have no shame before God when this occurs.

> For this reason a man shall leave his father and mother and be joined to his wife, and the two shall become one flesh. This is a great mystery, but I speak concerning Christ and the Church. (Ephesians 5:31-32)

When I was very young, I remember a certain situation that recurred over and over with my dad. As one of triplets, I was sort of known as the strong and feisty one. It seemed to me that of the threesome, my brother and sister did everything right while I was the one who messed up a lot and got in trouble for it. Though I was still young in my thought processes, I distinctly remember feeling the shame this brought to me as I said to myself, "Oh, Deborah, can you just do it right for once?"

In the midst of this accusation, after blowing it again, my dad would always call me to him. "Honey, come here," he would say. My insides would churn as I scolded myself inwardly for having messed up again; I would groan in resistance to the fact that I had to face my dad as a failure again. The last thing I wanted to do was walk over to him, feeling ashamed and embarrassed for my behavior. In my childish mind, I reasoned that my dad was mad at me. I assumed he would reject me because, once again, I didn't measure up. Without too much choice in the matter, I would reluctantly drag myself over to my dad.

On his knees, waiting patiently for me, he would put his arms around me and look at me eye to eye. Once again, just like every other time this happened, we would go through the same process. He would wrap his arms behind my back and I would press with all my little girl strength against them, shame causing me to want to distance myself from him. Unable to meet his eyes, my head would turn back and forth over and over to avoid this encounter.

Yet every time this happened, my dad did the same thing. He would ask, "Deborah, why are you resisting me?" Then, because I was so adamantly pressing against his arms, he would loosen them and I would fall to the ground. Each time, this fall would only add to my already stinging embarrassment, forcing me to stand up again to face my father. I have to get this over with, I would think, so I'd better just look him straight in the eye.

As I finally met his gaze, he said the same thing every time. The first thing out of his mouth was, "I love you. I love you." All my emotions and reasoning would argue. "No Dad, you can't love me now; I just messed up again. You are supposed to punish me, not embrace me. I can't receive your love right now. It's too much. Maybe when I do things right for a while and clean myself up, then you can hug me and tell me you love me. Right now I can't accept it; I've been too bad."

Though the process took a long time, my dad's persistence had a dramatic impact on me. I remember the day when this cycle was finally broken between us, and his affection won over my shame. This time, having messed up again and hearing him call me, I responded differently from all the times before. As my dad held me, for the first time I did not resist his embrace. And when he let go, I did not fall backward but simply relaxed in his arms. Excited and perhaps as surprised as I was, he said, "Deborah, look! I am holding you and you are not pulling away!" That day I realized I actually believed that my dad loved me—even liked me—in *spite of my stumbling and weakness, in spite of my failures.*—*Deborah Hiebert*

Deborah's story of resisting the embrace of her father is one that applies to all of humanity. Since Adam and Eve's sin (Genesis 3), it has been the story of mankind. After Adam and Eve sinned the first time, they recognized their nakedness and first encountered that crippling thing called shame. God then fashioned garments for them as covering (Genesis 3:21). Six thousand years later, God still offers a covering for our shame, this time through the sacrifice of His Son. God was and is fully determined to draw near to us in such a way that we would have no shame in our relationships with Him.

FINDING INTIMACY WITHOUT SHAME

Day after day, millions of human hearts are wounded in their search for intimacy. In their broken state, they pursue this God-given desire in ungodly ways, only to find shame and scorn for their efforts. Intimacy was not designed to be this way. In fact, it is possible to experience an intimacy with God and people that has no shame in it. Intimacy means so much more than a physical union. It is the empowering confidence people have in one another that allows them to share the deepest parts of their hearts—their hopes and dreams, their fears and failures, their feelings and frustrations.

There are times when my wife and I talk about the happenings of our days, the meetings we've been in, and the other people we have talked to, but eventually we move past the chit chat of people and places. The next question is invariably, "What are you really thinking?" We're not looking for a stream-of-consciousness discussion, we're asking the specifics: "What were you feeling during the events of the day? What were you excited about? What were you afraid of? What concerns arose in your heart? *What are your secrets?*" God knows the most secret aspects of our lives, especially the areas where we feel unknown, unnoticed, or misunderstood. He knows what we feel and what we fear. But He wants us to *invite* Him into the deep parts of our hearts each step of the way.

Most people hold back in these areas. They've had experiences where they've shared their deepest secrets with another person, sometimes even a spouse, and found out later that those secrets were betrayed and shared with others. Nothing hurts like an intimacy exposed. We learn that intimacy requires confidence. Telling our secrets involves more than simply transferring information. We can be sure that intimacy with Jesus is safe. He will not betray us, He will cover us. He will embrace us. He will keep our secrets.

And intimacy with Jesus is not a one-sided discussion. Jesus has secrets of His own. He has plans, feelings, and emotions that involve us. Intimacy involves our knowledge of His secrets as well. He desires to share with us what He is thinking. As Psalm 25:14 says, "The *secret of the* LORD is with those who fear Him…" Jesus desires to unveil His heart to us because He has confidence in us. It's amazing to consider, but the sorts of things Jesus wants to share with us are not mundane. They are the things nearest to His heart—things not even the highest-ranking angelic or demonic principalities and powers are aware of yet (Ephesians 3:10). Throughout eternity, Jesus will continue to tell us things that move His heart. God has called only the redeemed into intimacy with Him, not the angels. There is a boundary line the angels cannot cross in terms of experiencing God's heart, though they wish they knew the things God has reserved for intimacy with humans (1 Peter 1:12).

The geometry term *ray* is useful in understanding the idea of intimacy with Jesus. A ray is a line that has a beginning point, but no end. Moving from left to right on the number line, a ray begins and continues on in one direction eternally. Intimacy with Jesus is like that in a sense. Looking at a timeline, we can identify a point where we began to draw near to Him, to tell Him our secrets and listen carefully to His. This is the *beginning* of intimacy. It is different from human intimacy in that, while human intimacy is limited in scope, intimacy with God continues forever. There will be points in eternity, millions and billions of years from now, when Jesus will draw you near and say, "Let me tell you another secret..." He'll whisper it in your ear and it will be an entirely new thought to you. A billion years from now, He will still be a creator, and He will still be the lover of His people. The depth and length of His love is like a vast ocean that can never be exhausted.

There is nothing more exhilarating in our experience than our spirit touching this realm of intimacy with the Godhead. He is the uncreated God who is transcendent, infinite, and wholly other than, yet we have been invited to come near Him. While everything we know about His majesty would seem to make Him unapproachable, His heart draws us closer. It is the ultimate peasant-to-princess story.

> Having boldness to enter the Holiest by the blood
> of Jesus...let us draw near with a true heart in full
> assurance of faith... (Hebrews 10:19-22)

If you live in a neighborhood with other houses nearby, you may develop friendships with those neighbors that go beyond the casual wave over the hedge. At some point, you may be invited to their house for coffee. When that happens, the relationship shifts slightly. You were acquaintances when you were waving as you drove into your garage and shut the door. Having been invited into their house, you are much more likely to say you know them. In the same way, God is inviting us in—not to His kitchen, but into His very heart.

Human relationships that involve a measure of intimacy are complex. They are not impossible to navigate, but they certainly have more facets than the three-minute interaction we might have with the person who serves our hamburger at a fast-food restaurant. When we have been in deep relationship with someone for a period of time, we end up sharing the full range of our experience with them. The healthiest of marriages are defined by sharing in such a manner, and intimacy with Christ is based on this reality.

To know Christ and be known by Him means experiencing intimacy at levels we previously never imagined possible. When invited, He invades every place of our hearts and says, "I want to live here, too. I want to know all there is to know about you." He desires that all things hidden or private would be open before Him. In return, He reveals the hidden things of His heart to us.

INTIMACY IN OUR VICTORY AND PROSPERITY

There is nothing that a spouse enjoys more than seeing their mate succeed. Over the past few years, I have watched my wife, Diane, build a real estate business from the ground up. It has seen much success, helping to find housing for International House of Prayer missionaries and others around the Kansas City area. From the beginning, Diane determined to give the corporate profits of her business to support the house of prayer, blessing many on our staff who receive small amounts of monthly missionary stipends.

I know the long hours she has invested, late nights at a computer, the early morning coffee meetings with a wavering client, the phone calls from finance offices expecting her to produce documents out of thin air, over a cell phone, while she is shopping for groceries. When Diane comes home with a smile and says, "Today was a good day," I rejoice with her because I understand that today's good day was more than just a sweet set of circumstances. She's been working to produce today's good day for the last few years.

I have appreciation and joy for her victory because I have watched her work hard for it. I enjoy seeing what she is capable of. When we first discussed her plan to start a new business, we were positive it would be successful. But she has easily surpassed all our expectations, and I couldn't be happier for her.

What we feel about our spouse's success is a mere shadow of what God feels when one of us does well in our endeavors. By nature of being our Creator, He knows fully of what we are capable. But being also our Redeemer, He knows just as well how often we fall short of our capabilities. He is simultaneously our greatest coach, cheerleader, supporter, and defender.

God is like the football coach who looks past his first string of players to the scrawny ninth grader sitting on the bench. The poor kid looks pitiful. His jersey hangs to his knees, his shoulder pads dwarf his upper body, and his football pants are completely free of grass stains because he has yet to actually take to the field. Every Friday night under the lights, the kid sits and watches…and between calling plays in the big game, the coach watches him. The coach is watching in practice too. He sees that the young guy is the first on the field and the last to leave. He sees him studying his playbook when he could be doing pretty much anything else. The coach drives by the boy's house on Sunday afternoon to see him running plays in the back yard with his dad.

One Friday night, they walk back to the team bus after the game. The coach is tired from another long day. The kid is restless, having sat faithfully on the bench for hours. His pants are still spotless. The coach glances at the scrawny ninth grader and says, "You're going to make it, and you're going to make it big." The player is astonished. What does the coach know that no one else does? What could he possibly see that is unseen to the rest of the world? When God looks at you, even if you're not in the game yet, He sees the potential He invested in you. While He is fully aware of your failings, He is looking beyond them to the successes in your future. At a time when all indicators would suggest otherwise, He looks you squarely in the eye and says, "You're going to make it."

The coach who sees potential in the skinny ninth grader shares a special moment when that ninth grader is suddenly a high school senior and catches the touchdown pass to win the championship. The coach's joy transcends that moment to cover the whole of their relationship. The Lord celebrates the *now* in us, but he also celebrates the *then*, when we do well in the fullest sense. God celebrates us throughout the entire journey. Our intimacy with Him includes a far broader experience than what we are doing right now. He clearly sees where we are going in His grand plan for our lives.

It may seem unimportant that God celebrates our victories with us. One would expect that intimacy would be easy to grasp if you are successful, but human experience suggests otherwise. It's not always a given that those closest to you will celebrate your victories. Jesus alone knows the full implications of our true greatness in Him. As the football coach may see in us what we cannot see about ourselves, so the Lord sees much more in us than we could even consider. God alone fully understands our true nobility and the heights of our greatness in Him. He will experience greatness with us. *Jesus knows your greatness far better than you know it.* He alone really knows who we are.

Novelist Vicki Baum once wrote, "Fame always brings loneliness. Success is as ice-cold and lonely as the North Pole." When we are successful, all sorts of people gather around us and pat us on the back, but many do so with the intention of leveraging our success for their own good, or siphoning off our fame and fortune for their own purposes. They are not sharing our success out of intimacy, they are manipulating it for their opportunity. With a depth of sincerity unlike theirs, Jesus fully embodies what Paul wrote when he exhorted us to "rejoice with those who rejoice" (Romans 12:15). Like no human can, Jesus rejoices with us when we rejoice. His intimate knowledge of our potential for good and evil makes His joy that much more complete in those seasons when success is finally realized, both in this age and the age to come.

INTIMACY WITH US IN OUR PAIN AND STRUGGLE

Not all intimacy is centered on joy or celebration. In any relationship with profound transparency, there is pain to deal with.

We fail. We lose battles. We suffer because of our own sin as well as the sin of others. In those moments, Jesus lives out the second part of that passage in Romans, the call to "weep with those who weep" (Romans 12:15). Jesus alone knows the depths of our longings, dreams, and intentions to love Him. Even our failed intentions to love Him are seen and appreciated.

The two most powerful realities that move the human heart are beauty and pain. While we will forever be exhilarated with the beauty of Jesus, some of our greatest times of intimacy with Him will be as we fellowship amidst suffering (Philippians 3:10), as we endure pain and hardship. As there is in victory, there is an intimacy to be known and accepted in our suffering and failure. The pain of persecution and the pain of our failure actually serve as escorts to know and experience Jesus at more intimate levels. When our hearts are hurting and starving to be comforted, He will be most vivid in our experience, if we allow Him. When we are backed into a corner and He is our only way out, we enter into a sweet fellowship with Him in our struggle.

Jesus is our protector and our rescuer—the Man who went before us and gave everything for love is near to us and intimately knows our pain. During our darkest, hardest times, when most people draw away from us, He draws closer. He holds our hand, not as one who strives in vain to understand, but as one who has truly been there and who walks through each moment with us.

> For we do not have a High Priest who cannot sympathize with our weaknesses, but was in all points tempted as we are, yet without sin. Let us therefore come boldly to the throne of grace, that we may obtain mercy and find grace to help in time of need. (Hebrews 4:15-16)

> Though He was a Son, yet He learned obedience by the things which He suffered. And having been perfected, He became the author of eternal salvation to all who obey Him. (Hebrews 5:8-9)

The imperfect compassion we feel for others gives us some sort of grid for why Jesus helps us when circumstances are difficult. The newspaper's front-page photo of a newly-orphaned child brings forth a public outpouring of help. Money is donated, scholarships are provided, and offers of unconditional adoption come streaming in. Most seem to understand the idea of drawing near to the hurting in their times of great need. It's a very different scenario for the person who, by negligence or willful sin, makes a mess of their life. Human compassion often fails to make allowances for the father who flies into a rage and hurts his child or the lifelong drunk who, finally sober, walks out of the treatment program with the full intent of returning to his destructive behavior. We have no desire to suffer alongside those who bring suffering on themselves by their deliberate wrongdoing.

In those sorts of situations, where people are undeserving and have in fact rejected any sort of human kindness, the offer of intimacy with God seems to extend beyond human comprehension. God still extends an offer of mercy and grace to all, no matter how far they have wandered. Think of your own journey for a moment. Each of us, if totally honest, would have to acknowledge that Jesus has walked beside us through so much sin that it would be scandalous if revealed. In all of it, He covered us, protected us, and offered us a place to heal.

Perhaps no individual in the Bible displays this truth better than King David. Singled out as a man after God's own heart, David still managed to generate a fair amount of heartbreak for himself and his family. The chronicle of his life swings between great deeds for God and adultery, the founding of a prayer ministry, and raising murderous and fratricidal children. David exhibited characteristics of tenderness and underhandedness, often in the same chapter. There were probably times when David, the author of many of the psalms that speak eloquently of the nearness of God, probably felt very, very alone—but we know by studying the whole of his life that God drew near to him even in his failures. In fact, some of his most tender psalms were written in light of God's nearness to him when it was clear that he had failed.

In Psalm 51, David recounted his failure in detail, but closed the passage by pointing to what he had learned about the character of God—that even in our sin and struggle, the Lord consistently draws near to us.

> Deliver me from the guilt of bloodshed, O God, the God of my salvation, and my tongue shall sing aloud of Your righteousness...and my mouth shall show forth Your praise. For You do not desire sacrifice, or else I would give it; You do not delight in burnt offering. The sacrifices of God are a broken spirit, a broken and a contrite heart—these, O God, You will not despise. (Psalm 51:14-17)

God has walked us through every sin in our lives. He forgives us, feels our pain during failure, and protects us by not disclosing the vast majority of our sin. He knows our shameful deeds, yet believes in us and treats us with the honor we have not deserved or earned. Now *that* is intimacy with us in our struggle.

There is a dimension of intimacy extended from God's heart to ours, even when we are doing wrong. It is the most radical expression of forgiveness that has ever existed. While hanging on the cross in excruciating pain, humiliated before the crowd and in anguish over the coming separation from His Father, Jesus extended His love far beyond what any human could ever expect. The three words *"Father, forgive them"* (Luke 23:34) are the mark of a heart set toward intimacy, even in the face of unprecedented difficulty. They are the words spoken by One who deeply desires to partner with us on the deepest level, even on our darkest day. He truly does want to know us in both our successes and our failures. To embrace only the former while ignoring the latter is really not intimacy at all—it's convenience.

INTIMACY WITH US IN OUR SACRIFICES

In a scene from the film *Chariots of Fire*, when one character is trying to convince another to go beyond what would normally be expected of him, he tells him, "We are all called upon during times of war to make great sacrifices." One of our staff members, a father of three young boys, has used this line in all manner of circumstances when his children don't want to do something. Upon hearing them complain about tidying their rooms or mowing the yard, he deadpans, "Sorry boys, we are all called upon during times of war to make great sacrifices." The humor is lost on the children, but it does serve to remind them that sacrifice is not just demanded during trying times. We're all called to make sacrifices every day.

Living in relationship with other human beings whose desires often run contrary to our own means, we will be called upon regularly to make sacrifices for the greater good. These are the routine sacrifices of which life is made. We wash the dishes for each other. We allow the other to choose what we will eat or where we will eat it. We are gracious toward one another when preferences differ between us.

There is a second level of sacrifice, however, that goes beyond this. It's not a give-to-get sort of sacrifice. These sacrifices are not merely the back and forth, give and take of relational living, but rather the extension of Christ within us. It's not difficult to find sacrifice in the life of Christ. His very coming to earth in bodily form was a sacrifice we cannot completely comprehend (John 1:1-5). To move from His position at the right hand of the Father in heaven to become human, and then to *become sin* that we might become the righteousness of God (2 Corinthians 5:17), was a demonstration of sacrifice at which we will marvel forever. Angels must have stood in wonder and bewilderment as they watched Him descend to the earth and then go to the cross.

> He has appeared to put away sin by the sacrifice of Himself. (Hebrews 9:26)

Having paid that price, Jesus is uniquely qualified to encounter us intimately as we deal with the broad range of emotions we experience as we make significant sacrifices. From the
heroic struggles that may cost us our lives, to the humbling daily
sacrifices, we receive strength in knowing Jesus recognizes them
all. He knows all of them in a way we can't articulate; He knows
the pain of what it costs us far better than even we do.

You may be making a sacrifice right now. Perhaps you're
holding your tongue as rumors fly around you. You would be
justified in defending yourself, but the Holy Spirit is impressing
you not to. Perhaps you're in a marriage that has been far less
than God intended. Your best friends have offered you all sorts
of justification for ending it, but you know God wants you to
persevere right now. Maybe you are being called upon to make
a financial sacrifice because someone you know needs funds. You
know this will mean that you will go without some things.

In these moments of legitimate sacrifice on our part, we
come nearer to the character of Jesus. This explains why the
fury of hell seems to be unleashed on us in these moments. All
kinds of feelings enter our hearts. *Is this really worth it? Does anyone
even know that I'm paying the price for this?* In these moments, having
made the initial sacrifice with willing hearts, many find themselves wavering in their resolve to follow through. While they're
sacrificing on the outside, on the inside they want to stand up
and scream, "I'm sacrificing, but I don't like it and I want the
whole world to know!"

Throughout history, the heart of Jesus has drawn near to
those who have known sacrifice. From the martyrs of the first
century to the home-schooling mom of this century, His eye has
been attracted to those who have given without expecting to be
noticed by other people. He sees our hearts and knows all; this
encourages us to go on. In intimacy with Him, we find strength
to continue. The frustration passes as we confess, "I can do this.
I can do all things through Christ who strengthens me." Eventually, through the intimacy with God that accompanies our giving, we will find a certain joy in sacrificially pouring ourselves

out. Paul knew intimacy with Jesus in times of sacrifice. The fiery little Jewish evangelist who once spent his days persecuting Christians found himself as the apostolic leader over many fledgling Christian congregations. He was called upon to give of himself; his energy, his time, even his emotions, were taxed by these believers.

> Yes, and if I am being poured out as a drink offering on the sacrifice and service of your faith, I am glad and rejoice with you all. (Philippians 2:17)

> I also count all things loss for the excellence of the knowledge of Christ Jesus my Lord, for whom I have suffered the loss of all things, and count them as rubbish, that I may gain Christ...that I may know Him and...the fellowship of His sufferings, being conformed to His death... (Philippians 3:8-10)

Paul discovered an intrinsic value in intimacy with Christ— joy in sacrifice. Jesus wants to come alongside us in those moments when we wonder if anyone even realizes what sacrifices we are making, and give us joy in the moment so that we, like Paul, can be glad and rejoice as we are being poured out for others. Intimacy with Jesus in sacrifice is by no means limited to this age. In the age to come, He will recall each sacrifice we made throughout our Christian lives. He will surprise us as He retells times of giving we have long forgotten and how He felt about us when we were giving ourselves to others for His sake.

> For God is not unjust to forget your work and labor of love which you have shown toward His name, in that you have ministered to the saints... (Hebrews 6:10)

> "Whoever gives one of these little ones only a cup of cold water in the name of a disciple, assuredly, I say to you, he shall by no means lose his reward." (Matthew 10:42)

INTIMACY IN KNOWING THE PASSIONS OF OUR HEART

The One who wove us together in our mother's womb and who sees our greatness throughout all of eternity is the One who is leading our life now. He planned our prophetic destiny and knows our unique design, the way we have been formed and fashioned, as only a creator can.

> O LORD, You have searched me and known me. You know my sitting down and my rising up; You understand my thought afar off. You comprehend my path...and are acquainted with all my ways. For there is not a word on my tongue, but behold, O LORD, You know it altogether...Such knowledge is too wonderful for me...For You formed my inward parts; You covered me in my mother's womb...For I am fearfully and wonderfully made...My frame was not hidden from You, when I was made in secret, and skillfully wrought...Your eyes saw my substance, being yet unformed. And in Your book they all were written, the days fashioned for me, when as yet there were none of them. (Psalm 139:1-16)

The Lord sees the end from the beginning. With intimate knowing, He understands what excites us and what we are passionate about. He knows the depths of our longings and our greatest dreams. He knows why we are passionate and how this zeal is a glorious part of who He made us to be.

Next time you're around a group of people of varying ages, conduct a little experiment. Ask the children what they want to be when they grow up. The answers will fly fast and furiously: a policeman, a fireman, a ballerina, a scientist, a cowboy, a doctor, and usually about half a dozen astronauts and race car drivers. It seems that they don't need a second to think about it. In fact, they already have thought about it and they're not ashamed to announce it. They are quick to declare their intentions, no matter how far out they are. Next, move to the adults and ask what they want to do most in life. Prepare yourself for blank stares and stammering lips. Most of them will struggle to verbalize anything, and when they do, it will be some generic non-answer like, "I just want to do whatever God gives me to do." While there is a measure of wisdom in being willing to do what God gives us to do, the answer itself usually communicates a bit of uncertainty, insecurity, and even detachment. Some will give the impression that they never really think much about what they want to do. But God thinks a lot about what He created us for. The truth is these adults have thought hard, lost many hours of sleep, and prayed often about what they want to do. Nevertheless, when asked to verbalize it, they get tongue-tied. Why is this?

There is sometimes a false piety or false humility in denying the passions of our hearts. It has its origins in the extreme, legalistic fringe of the holiness movement. We're conditioned to believe that if something is pleasurable, it must be wrong. If there is something we would really love to do, then it must stand in direct opposition to God's plan for the cosmos. *God* does not equal *fun*. Or *joy*. Or *pleasure*. As a result, the same person who would have rattled off a half dozen life plans at the age of eight, suddenly becomes quiet as a mouse when the idea of destiny is raised once they're past the age of twenty-five. *Destiny? Oh my, never. Not me. I just want to serve the Lord.* What if you could do both? What if you could reach for the dreams within your heart and serve God wholeheartedly at the same time in this age and the age to come? It can be done. In fact, you probably can't fully do the latter without doing the former.

Psalm 37:4 says: "Delight yourself also in the Lord, and He shall give you the desires of your heart." This verse has been interpreted a number of ways. I've heard it taught that if you love God wholeheartedly, He will drop these little blessings your way—that car you've always promised yourself, for instance, or a place in the sun, white picket fence, everything. The logical extension of this train of thought is some sort of big swap meet with God, a "pray for pay" plan that puts Him in the role of a heavenly Santa Claus rather than a loving Father. I've also heard that if you delight yourself in Him, He will supernaturally implant desires in your heart that are actually His. While there is a good rationality for this, and of course He does plant desires in our hearts, holding narrowly to this perspective makes God seem like some puppeteer of desire, who tricks you into doing His will by convincing you it's what you want. Taking this idea too far produces an image of a God who brainwashes you into thinking you should be joyful about His underhandedness.

I think there's a third way of looking at intimacy with Christ as expressed through the passions of our hearts. What if, at the moment we became a person, we were hard-wired for certain pursuits? Could it be that He has, in fact, implanted the desires of our hearts within us, not in the form of some conditional contract, but as extensions of who we really are?

There's a reason you feel a pure sense of pleasure when you do certain things. Perhaps they are the things you were truly made to do. The preacher who is as fulfilled preaching to five people as to five thousand was made to preach. The musician who is as content playing to an empty prayer room as she is to a room full of worshipers, was made to play. The businessperson who gets great satisfaction from a job done well was created for that labor. God placed those desires in their hearts and when they express them, He draws especially near to them. God intimately knows what is in each of us. He totally comprehends the passions that He specifically designed for our hearts. When we express them, He has joy in His heart, and He means for us to experience some of this joy.

Eric Liddell was on the British Olympic Track and Field team during the 1924 Olympics. The story of his athletic career and how it dovetailed into his life on the mission field is well known as told in the movie *Chariots of Fire*. In the film, when questioned about his decision to run, he answers, "I believe God made me for a purpose, but He also made me fast. And when I run, I feel His pleasure." To share in the passions of another's heart is an extremely personal form of intimacy, and leads us to reverse the question: Jesus, what are the passions of Your heart? What can I do that will allow me to feel Your pleasure? When we believe He shares our enthusiasm for certain things, we begin to ask more intentionally what He takes joy in. In knowing that He shares passions particular to our personalities, we desire to share more of His passions, His personality. It is the natural extension of intimacy; we begin to feel more at one with Him.

Intimacy without shame is a lost concept for most people. They have lived their entire lives in relationships that were more a trade-off than anything resembling intimacy. Anything they encountered approaching intimacy usually involved the shame of knowing it was happening outside of a covenant relationship. To a world full of people who are longing for intimacy without shame, Jesus says, "I am here to meet you. I will rejoice with you in your successes. I will weep with you during your times of failure and heartache. I will see and understand your sacrifices, and I will celebrate and affirm the passions that make you unique in time and eternity. I will be truly intimate with you—I will know you, and you will know Me, and there will be no shame in it."

CHAPTER SIX

The Longing to Be Wholehearted

They had gathered together with a clear purpose, and they did not intend to be thwarted. This teacher from Galilee had been stirring things up for a while now; it was time to teach Him a lesson. It was growing increasingly difficult to maintain control of the people who heard Jesus preach. The Pharisees had their defenses up. They knew that earlier that same day He had silenced the Sadducees with His mastery of the Scripture and they did not want the same thing to happen to them. According to plan, the brightest among them made the first move. A lawyer, seasoned in the law of the land as well as the teaching of the prophets, asked a question to test Him. "Teacher, which is the great commandment in the law?"

All eyes turned to the Teacher. He paused for a moment—not because He was searching for the answer, but to allow the weight of the question to hang in the air. After a moment, He spoke.

> Jesus said to him, "'You shall love the LORD your God with all your heart, with all your soul, and with all your mind.' This is the first and great commandment. And the second is like it: 'You shall love your neigh-

bor as yourself.' On these two commandments hang
all the Law and the Prophets." (Matthew 22:37-40)

A murmur ran through the crowd. These were not new ideas
to them; they were taken directly from their own Scriptures
(Deuteronomy 6:5; Leviticus 19:18). The stir came not from the
words themselves, but from the authority with which they were
spoken. Jesus wasn't just quoting a Scripture or giving a regur-
gitated answer to pass a test. He was prophesying about how
Israel would respond to God in the future. "You *shall* love God
with all your heart," He proclaimed over the people of Israel.
This statement is not just an informational statement but a prophetic oracle from heaven: the time is coming when followers
of God will follow Him with wholehearted love, not mindless
ritual or casual indifference. His people will be people who love
Him radically and passionately. Yes, God will have a people who
love Him with all their energy. Today, the Holy Spirit is emphasizing this truth worldwide: "Love the Lord your God with all
your heart."

God will restore the first commandment to first place in the
Body of Christ. As this happens, we will give our deepest affection to God. The "joy of lovesickness" is exhilarating. There
is a joy and power in being lovesick for Jesus. Loyal, holy love
frees us from the burnout of spiritual boredom. Boredom makes
us vulnerable to destruction, but God imparts to us the power
to be passionate, because He is a passionate God. To love God
with all of our strength speaks of loving Him without any of
our energy defiled, depleted, or diminished. We cannot function
properly until we have passionately given our hearts to God in
this way. Halfheartedness diminishes our glory as human beings. We long to love God wholeheartedly, and have no de-
filement or compromise in our hearts or lives. God gave us the
longing to love Him wholeheartedly. And when we allow Him
and ask Him to, God empowers us to be wholehearted and then,
in response to our wholeheartedness, loves and gives Himself to
us with all His heart.

We soar to the heights of our human potential only when we fully love God. Today's weary Church needs a vision of the pleasures of loving God. It was the desire to see this vision established in the Church that prompted me to write *The Pleasures of Loving God* in 2000. God's insistence on wholeheartedness towards Him is not for His own gratification. He is not an insecure narcissist looking to His created beings for affirmation. He knows exactly who He is and of what He is capable. His insistence on wholeheartedness is for our benefit. Loving God with all of our hearts allows us to experience the heights and fullness of what it means to be human.

Our emotional capacity for love is immense. We were created for love, and God will empower us to receive His love, love Him in return, and love others. It takes God to love God, and it takes our receipt of God's supernatural power to give us the capacity to love Him. Thus, the supernatural work of His Spirit empowers us to walk out full obedience. Paul described it this way: "The love of God has been poured out in our hearts by the Holy Spirit" (Romans 5:5). The Holy Spirit pours God's affection into the human heart regardless of personality type, history of bondage, woundedness, or brokenness. It's a supernatural activity that transcends the human condition.

This graceful impartation of love is the only way we will be able to live as the equally-yoked Bride of Jesus throughout eternity. Our primary reward is in having the power to love. Our desire for God is His gift to us. Our reward is to feel and receive love, and then to reciprocate it by the power of God. Our lives are not to be measured by how big our ministries grow, but by how much we have grown in loving God and subsequently loving others. Even in this age we can enjoy the great reward of being empowered to love as the primary preoccupation of our lives. It's a pleasure beyond compare. David spoke of his delight in wholeheartedness when he wrote, "I delight to do Your will, O my God, and Your law is within my heart" (Psalm 40:8).

GOD'S FIERY EMOTIONS

God's capacity for burning affection is one of the most unique aspects of His character. To be deeply loved and to deeply love in return is one of the unique qualities of the human spirit. This capacity for affection brings us to unimaginable heights of glory, but it can also be our downfall, bringing us to agonizing depths of perversion. An individual's capacity for burning desire, if refused, releases a terrifying capacity for destruction. Emotions can bring us to heights far beyond the angels if we say yes to God's grace, but to the lowest places of darkness if we say no to it.

Exodus 20:5 says, "For I, the LORD your God, am a jealous God." God has jealous, fiery emotions for us and has created us to have the same emotions in response to Him. One example of this is seen in the jealous zeal that Phinehas had for God in the generation of Moses.

> Israel...began to commit harlotry with the women of Moab. They invited the people to the sacrifices of their gods, and the people ate and bowed down to their gods. So Israel was joined to Baal of Peor, and the anger of the LORD was aroused against Israel. One of the children of Israel came and presented to his brethren a Midianite woman...when Phinehas...saw it, he rose from among the congregation and took a javelin in his hand; and he went after the man of Israel into the tent and thrust both of them through...so the plague was stopped among the children of Israel...Then the LORD spoke to Moses, saying: "Phinehas...has turned back My wrath from the children of Israel, because he was zealous with My zeal among them, so that I did not consume the children of Israel in My zeal." (Numbers 25:1-11)

HOLY ROMANCE

As noted, the gospel's message of holiness is not centered around gritting our teeth and *trying* harder. Instead it brings people into what I call the "holy romance of the gospel." This is not a term found in Scripture, but one I've used for years to describe what happens in the human heart. The words *Trinity* and *rapture* are not biblical terms either, but they are perfect to describe important biblical truths. When I speak of "holy romance," I am referring to what happens when a person's heart is exhilarated by receiving holy love from Jesus and feeling holy love toward Him. This is a love that causes human beings to sacrifice greatly in any number of areas in their lives, even in the face of death.

When Paul reflected on his sacrifices for God, he testified that what he gave up was rubbish compared to the glory of knowing Jesus. He gave up a brilliant career with incredible financial advantages, but he counted it as the heap of ashes he knew it ultimately was. This is the epitome of what I mean by holy romance. Some fall into serious error by mistakenly assuming sexual overtones are appropriate in their spiritual relationship with Jesus, in the name of a supposed holy romance. This is Satan's deception to undermine the development and proper placement of the first commandment in a person's life. What this romance is speaking of is a heart burning like John the Baptist's heart and like Paul's heart. It speaks of what Revelation 12:11 describes: "And they overcame him by the blood of the Lamb and by the word of their testimony, and they did not love their lives to the death" (Revelation 12:11).

When Jesus is our magnificent obsession, material and peripheral rewards become secondary. We become powerful and fearless in the grace of God when our primary purpose of loving God is fulfilled. I call this "the anointing of the first commandment." It is our greatest reward in this life. We carry this with us wherever we go, even during dry seasons. From this perspective, life looks totally different, because no matter what happens, a song fills our hearts, stirs us, and our inner man is tender toward God. When Jesus is our primary reward, we can lose everything for the gospel—go to prison, suffer physically, be tortured—and still be successful.

> But what things were gain to me, these I have counted
> loss for Christ. Yet indeed I also count all things loss
> for the excellence of the knowledge of Christ Jesus my
> Lord, for whom I have suffered the loss of all things,
> and count them as rubbish, that I may gain Christ.
> (Philippians 3:7-8)

Paul's life as a follower of Jesus was filled with hardship (2 Corinthians 11:23-28), but in the midst of it, he greatly loved Jesus and considered his sufferings as not worthy of being compared to what God gave him in his relationship with Jesus. Paul counted his difficulties as momentary light afflictions. He wrote,

> For our light affliction, which is but for a moment,
> is working for us a far more exceeding and eternal
> weight of glory... (2 Corinthians 4:17)

> For I consider that the sufferings of this present time
> are not worthy to be compared with the glory which
> shall be revealed in us. (Romans 8:18)

Holy romance speaks of finding our glory in the ability to walk in holy love and hundredfold obedience to Jesus. No sacrifice will be too great when our hearts are set on fire. We are all fascinated by stories of wholeheartedness. Whether it's a story of an athlete, the stories of scaling mountains or reaching the unreachable stars, we love stories of people who give everything, because they are stories that resonate with how we were made to live! There is nothing more compelling or attractive than desire combined with commitment that goes above and beyond the norm.

Hollywood has made billions of dollars from movies trumpeting courageous, fiery love. Every love story through the ages has done the same, but people still flock to the theater to see the same story line over and over. Why? Because something in us longs for love that knows no boundaries, a love that embraces any sacrifice in pursuing the one it loves. From *Romeo and Juliet* to *Casablanca*, the classic tales through the ages have been those that espouse a radical love at any cost. All too often they are tragic in conclusion, because that is all we know in striving after earthly shadows of true love. But they communicate the truth that life itself is only worthwhile if the heart burns with love. And we devour it. We rejoice to see passion in others and we celebrate those who love with their whole hearts, because we love to love in this way. The reason we love to love in this way is that God designed us to love in this way. This is the glory of the gospel.

No pleasure is more intense than the pleasure that comes when God communicates His love, His passion, His heart to the human spirit. It is life at its best. Such tender moments with God cause life, love, and spiritual vitality to resonate deep within us. Of course, we do not experience an unbroken sense of God's love in this life. Such dramatic touches of God's presence will wax and wane. Only in heaven will we enjoy the continual ecstasy of His presence. During my tender moments with God, I say to myself and to God, "Oh, yes, I like life. Life is good!" As God pours His love into me, that same love flows from me back to Him. As I love Him in return, greater revelation of His affection and beauty comes to me, and the cycle just gets richer and richer. Even so, there is a greater, deeper love that is coming to the hearts of people in the age to come.

As the events that will ultimately lead to the Great Tribulation increase pressure everywhere, the Church will only be made ready as she is empowered through holy romance with God. The Church will interpret the difficulties of the last days, even martyrdom, through a lens of love. As God's temporal judgments disrupt the world and its inhabitants, the end-time Bride of Christ will see God's hand of mercy and goodness manifested. The Church must have vision for this holy romance to allow her to make sense of Jesus the Judge as He brings judgment to the nations of the world in the Great Tribulation. We will not understand God's judgments if we don't have a revelation that they come as a result of the Bridegroom's love for His Bride.

THE MISSING DIMENSION OF OUR REDEMPTION

The Reformers and their successors radically transformed Christianity by reviving an essential truth of the gospel—we are justified by faith alone through grace alone. What a liberating experience it was for people to understand that the gift of righteousness could be received simply by faith. It was like coming out of darkness into the daylight. Salvation involves a glorious exchange in which Christ takes our sin and guilt, and we take on His righteousness. I love the doctrines of salvation, sanctification, and adoption that highlight our legal position in Christ. I believe they are a vital dimension of the preaching of the cross and are foundational to a healthy walk with God.

Unfortunately, some of reformed evangelicalism has become rigid and scholastic in reducing a relationship with God to our legal standing with Him. The gospel involves far more than God stamping *accepted* on our passport to heaven. Yes, that's good news, but that is not the whole of the story of the good news: God's heart is ravished and filled with delight for His people (Song of Solomon 4:9). In the Song of Solomon the bride understands this about the king, saying, "I am my beloved's, and his desire is toward me" (Song of Solomon 7:10). What a statement! Out of a heart consumed with this revelation of God's desire, the bride proclaims that she belongs to the king, and why.

In addition to our legal purification before God, salvation includes intimacy with God, a relationship that involves the receiving and giving of deep affection between our hearts and God's. As God communicates His longing and affections for us, we respond in a similar way. As John said, we love Him because He first loved us (1 John 4:19). An intellectual understanding of the legal aspects alone is not enough. Why? Because we are intended and want to have more passion for God than we do for the lawyer who gets us out of a speeding fine. We must understand what God feels for us; the revelation of the loving, passionate God must pulsate at the core of all our ministries, whether teaching others how to receive salvation, ministering to the sick, or leading a home group. Although God is totally self-sufficient, He desires our love. He, who has no need of us, abounds in His desire for us.

The first commandment must be first in our lives or we will live in boredom and be vulnerable to Satan. The human heart does not work properly in halfheartedness. It will be passive and therefore vulnerable to many destructive lusts. To be emotionally whole, we must live wholeheartedly. Some counseling ministries in the Church fall into deception as they attempt to help people find emotional wholeness without insisting that their clients live in wholeheartedness with God. Wholeheartedness is necessary for our emotional health. Many believers try to find security and happiness in the grace of God without being abandoned to God. They look for a way to make grace reinforce their carnal lifestyles.

THE POWER OF LIVING BY LOVE

Living by love and finding strength in God's embrace will revolutionize our Christian lives. People who are in love give up a lot less often than those who are not in love. Being in love gives us strength and tenacity when we're tempted to let go. Being a lover of God not only reduces burnout, it also reduces temptation, because we find less satisfaction in sin. Much of the sin in the Body of Christ is a wrong response to pain, fear, and the need for comfort. Sin is a false comfort that people use as a prop to get them through seasons of pain. Many get into sin because they feel beaten up and abandoned by God and others. They reach out for immediate comfort in status, financial gain, or wrong expressions of sexuality. Those who are spiritually satisfied are not sinless, but they do sin *less*.

Being a lover of God reduces the amount of strife in our relationships: happy people fight less. All of us are slandered at some point in our lives—and I do not always respond rightly to such attacks. However, when I experience God's presence, I fight people a lot less and I respond to hard situations in more godly ways.

In 2 Corinthians 5:14, Paul wrote, "For the love of Christ compels us, because we judge thus: that if One died for all, then all died." In writing this, he was motivated by love for God. It worked in him and empowered him in all he did. It is the power of living in godliness. I encourage people to focus on enjoying God more, not trying harder to overcome sin. Many people are driven by fear instead of by affection for God. I become far steadier in my commitments when the first commandment is in first place in my life. Satan wants to undermine our love for Jesus by sidetracking and diverting us from the simplicity of undistracted love and devotion (2 Corinthians 11:3). Satan attempts to lead us astray from knowing Jesus' love and kindness to us and responding back to Him in kind. When we do not feel cherished by God in our weakness, we begin to be distracted from pure devotion.

THE DESIRE OF JESUS' HEART

It's useful to ponder what Jesus really wants. Jesus is the Son of God, present at creation and sitting forever at the right hand of the Father. It's hard to imagine Him longing for much of anything. What do we give the God who has everything? Only what He wants...and what He wants is our wholehearted love. Jesus Himself expressed what He wants: "...that the love with which You loved Me may be in them, and I in them." (John 17:26).

God wants voluntary lovers. Jesus is not looking to abduct a bride from a foreign tribe and haul her off against her will. He is intent on winning her wholly to Himself with her full agreement. In this passage, Jesus was in essence saying to the Father, "You said there would be a people who would love Me as You love Me, Father." Jesus was asking the Father to supernaturally impart the Father's love for the Son to us, creating voluntary lovers who are so overcome with love that it can only be compared to the way the Father loves the Son. This prayer will be answered more and more fully as the first commandment prevails in the lives of God's people worldwide. The Father's holy zeal and love for Jesus will fill the hearts of God's people. Imagine the effect of affection for and fascination with Jesus that is the overflow of the love the Father has for His Son. That is what Jesus prayed for us to receive.

In John 17, Jesus prayed the High Priestly Prayer that ended His ministry before He went to the garden of Gethsemane and finally to the cross. Everything Jesus prayed for is, in essence, a prophetic promise that cannot fail. He did not pray amiss; everything the Lord asked of the Father in this prayer will come to pass. I think it should be the prayer of prayers, the model prayer in our desire to grow in intercession. The Church will love Jesus as intensely as the Father loves Him. The passionate God will give us the power to be passionate. The love the Father has for His Son will be imparted to us, and we will not be satisfied until we passionately give ourselves back to Him. There is nothing more satisfying than being lovesick for God and satisfied in it.

The Father is committed to seeing a people awakened in their affections for Jesus; a people who see and feel what God sees and feels when He looks at His beloved Son. The Father is zealous about having a passionate Church that loves Jesus as He loves Jesus. He will not fail in this. A revival of the intimate knowledge of God is coming, and as a result, the Church will be filled with holy passion for the Son. Divinely inspired intimacy and passion are on the Holy Spirit's agenda, because they are the prayers of Jesus.

WE LONG FOR WHOLEHEARTEDNESS

We started the International House of Prayer with interns, with young people who came to give their all to God. Earlier I mentioned that in the years following their arrival, many of them fell in love and got married. Next came the wave of those young couples having children. We're at the phase now where we have many toddlers in our community. Having grown up in the environment of a house of prayer, they think it's normal to spend time in the prayer room. Being the children of worship leaders and prayer leaders, these little guys often come to do real spiritual business in the prayer room. They sing at the top of their lungs, dance, even pray on the microphone occasionally. They also sleep. In fact, if they're not doing one, they're usually doing another. If they're awake, they're wholeheartedly praising. We were created to live wholeheartedly before God. This strikes a chord in our innermost being, because this is how it is supposed to be; we know in our hearts this is what we were made for.

WHAT WHOLEHEARTEDNESS LOOKS LIKE

Many people come to the realization that God wants them to live a wholehearted life, so they take the plunge, make the commitment to Jesus, and even declare it to those around them. "I'm going to do it right this time. I'm going to be wholehearted with the Lord!" They are undoubtedly committed to being something, but may have no idea as to what it will look like. After six months of discouragement, they quit. They were sincere at the beginning, but lacking a model, they failed. In looking for a model of wholeheartedness, we need to look no further than the words of Jesus and recognize that our love for God must be expressed in obedience and not merely religious sentiment.

> "He who has My commandments and keeps them,
> it is he who loves Me...if anyone loves Me, he will
> keep My word..." (John 14:21-23)

Many people today are stumbling through their Christian walks with little experience of God. The message that is popular today promises more comfort without really challenging us to die to our flesh in our pursuit of absolute obedience. Our programs go on and on, completely lacking in power and impact, even growing bigger, and we assume that more people doing our "church thing" is good, even if our church thing is shallow, powerless, and devoid of passion. Like Samson, some of these churches feel they're at the top of their game spiritually, but are entirely unaware that God's presence and power has left them. As for the few that are aware, they're not even alarmed by it. They're convinced they had a little bit of it once, and that was good enough.

Halfheartedness with God is a horrible way to live. Halfhearted followers have too much of God to enjoy sin and too much sin to enjoy God. They are left somewhere in between with a serious spiritual dichotomy, and are usually quite miserable. While giving verbal assent to the superiority of the things of God, they give themselves much more fully to things that feed their flesh. Until we come to a place of wholeheartedness before God, we will never be effective or satisfied.

Frighteningly large percentages of the Body of Christ live halfhearted lives and accept it as normal. In Africa, where centuries of superstition and animism pervade, a radical Christian culture of prayer and fasting is growing. In the former Soviet Union, Christian believers are rising to places of influence and bringing their outspoken faith with them. China's believers are evangelizing and teaching new believers to live out their faith in the midst of persecution. All the while, American believers attend services patterned after their favorite television shows because nothing else can hold their attention for an hour. Why the drastic difference? Are the souls of the Chinese more resilient than Americans' souls? Are we being lulled to sleep by our own freedoms and successes? Surely we are made of the same stuff as believers worldwide, at least at the core. So how do we explain our apparent spiritual shallowness? What is behind so much half-hearted Christianity in the Western world?

I believe that part of the answer lies in the lack of any challenge to a life of wholeheartedness in our love and obedience to Jesus. Instead of hearing the normal Christian lifestyle defined so clearly in the Sermon on the Mount (Matthew 5-7) being preached, we are being given a message that is so watered down, the early believers in the Book of Acts would hardly recognize it. Today, many churchgoers are in the dangerous position of thinking this weak, watered-down approach to Jesus is real Christianity. It leaves them disillusioned in their day-to-day routines and stagnant in their spiritual lives, despite their weekly attendance in a local church. They are not lacking in core beliefs; they are lacking in vision and leadership. They are lacking in ability to see the picture of what wholeheartedness looks like when it's authentically lived out.

FASTING: ENHANCING SPIRITUAL PLEASURE

Love for God will make you "spiritually violent" for the kingdom of God; violent enough to endure persecution and even martyrdom. The Bible says the violent will take the kingdom by *force* (Matthew 11:12). A holy, violent love will make us live very differently before God. The passion behind this love is so strong, so violent, it will keep us from ever quitting or giving up. Let our hearts be molded into the heart of a lovesick bride and let us become individuals like John the Baptist, who fasted and lived in the desert in order to grow in his love for God (Matthew 11:18).

Our greatest pleasure comes by feasting on the person of Jesus. Our pursuit of intimacy with Him involves fasting food because it brings our body into its proper relationship with the life of the Spirit. As we fast food, we seek to feast on Jesus. Fasting does not restrain our pleasure, it enhances it.

Does this sound odd? It's because we live in a culture that thinks backwards. We have been taught that we will experience more life if we pamper our bodies. This is wrong, even on a purely natural level. Though our souls live in physical bodies, they were not designed to be slaves to physical pleasures and passions. If we want our spirit man to gain ascendancy over our flesh, we must deliberately silence the compulsions of our natural man. Only in properly denying some of our fleshly passions, can both the physical and emotional aspects of our person experience the superior pleasures of life in the Spirit. Additionally, God actually ordained that fasting would strengthen our physical bodies, not weaken them. We typically approach fasting as if we are waging war on our bodies, when in fact fasting is intended to release warfare in the spirit realm. It is the world's system that wages war against us, both physically and spiritually. God created our physical bodies for fasting. Fasting is given of God to serve and help our natural frames enter into the highest places in the experience of God.

Consider also Mary of Bethany, the woman who broke the alabaster box of perfume. Mary was not an apostle. She was never famous, never wrote a book, never led a conference, and didn't say much as far as we are told. Her passionate love was in secret; she just loved the Lord ferociously in secret. She took all she had, all her earthly treasure, that alabaster box filled with spikenard worth thirty thousand dollars, and lavishly, extravagantly poured it upon the One she loved.

> A woman came to Him having an alabaster flask of very costly fragrant oil, and she poured it on His head as He sat at the table. But when His disciples saw it, they were indignant, saying, "Why this waste? For this fragrant oil might have been sold for much and given to the poor." But when Jesus was aware of it, He said to them, "Why do you trouble the woman? For she has done a good work for Me...Assuredly, I say to you, wherever this gospel is preached in the whole world, what this woman has done will also be told as a memorial to her." (Matthew 26:7-13)

Something magnificent happens when human beings recognize the value of the pleasure of this romance and choose it instead of the dust of this world. Something amazing happens when we look at God and see His incredible worth. Something superb happens when we fall in love with Him and put our own gold in the dust. We find gold in Him. God will reward those who consider Him to be their highest gold forever.

> "If you return to the Almighty...you will remove iniquity far from your tents. Then you will lay your

gold in the dust...yes, the Almighty will be your
gold...for then you will have your delight in the Almighty." (Job 22:23-26)

HOLDING ON TO JESUS WITH ALL OF OUR HEARTS

When I found the one I love...I held him and would
not let him go. (Song of Songs 3:4)

In this verse we see that, after the Bride's struggle of searching without finding, going into the city even in the face of her
fear, again seeking for Jesus to no avail, receiving help even from
the watchmen, Jesus renews His presence to her. She finds the
One she loves. He answers her persistent striving to find Him.
She presses through the dark night until finally she finds the
blessing of His presence. Suddenly, she is in His embrace. Upon
finding Him, she holds Him and refuses to let Him go. Her
painful season of struggle causes a godly tenacity to arise within
her and she clings to Him with all of her might. A tremendous
resolve arises from her spirit and she sees that, on the scale of
worth, finding Jesus far outweighs the cost of obedience. Whatever it takes, she desires to remain close to Him, unhindered by
her compromise.

This new, holy embrace is fierce, deep, and intimate, and it
is part of what God desired to bring about all along. Jesus knew
her struggle would ignite this deep fire in her. One of His main
purposes in withholding His presence was to bring her into the
fervency of this fiery clinging. With newly-found zeal and conviction she embraces Him, vowing to never again let Him go. As
an expression of her gratitude and her desperation for Him, she
deeply resolves to never again consciously compromise by doing anything that hinders the development of her love for God.
Mature love is birthed in "holy violence" that continues to hold
on to Jesus. This speaks of a resolute clinging to Jesus in a life of
prayer until the deeper things of His heart are attained. For the
responsive heart, these God-ordained seasons create spiritual
violence, an unquenchable resolution empowered by the Spirit

of God to do the will of God. This holy violence in turn creates abandonment, a resolve to give up anything that gets in the way of intimacy with God. A holy commitment arises within to live constantly in the state of being in love with God.

The Song of Solomon, the King's song to His Bride, needs to be taught and sung with revelation and power. It will wash and restore the Church as it prophetically calls her forth to holy passion. It can be interpreted on different levels; either as the historical story of King Solomon wooing and wedding a young shepherdess, or allegorically, where it presents Israel as God's espoused Bride in the same way the Church is also pictured as the Bride of Christ in the New Testament. Some say it describes the love of an actual man for his wife. Others see it as a true story written in symbolic language with spiritual meaning for believers today. Personally, I believe the Holy Spirit interprets the book to the Church in all these different ways and we can learn from each of them; but I want to share the way the book has most edified me.

In this love song from heaven, I picture the maiden as the young maturing Church, the Bride of Christ. I see a clear spiritual progression in the eight chapters of the Song of Solomon. It is a divine pattern that reveals the progression of holy passion in the heart of the Bride as she is wooed by the beauty and splendor of her glorious King. There are at least two wonderful benefits from meditating upon this great prophetic song. First, the Holy Spirit unveils to us the passions and pleasures in the personality of the Son of God. This insight into the heart of Jesus captures our hearts in a fresh way, energizes us, and opens us to new depths of passion for Him. Second, as we meditate upon the Song of Solomon we identify our present position in the divine progression of Christian maturity.

While I had always felt a deep longing to be consumed with desire for God, I remember a specific morning in my office when the Lord called me to proclaim the Song of Solomon and the message of the Bride of Christ. I had prayed often, studied the Scriptures, and surrounded myself with great teachers and preachers by reading many books. But on that day as I knelt to pray in my office, little did I expect to receive a new direction that would result in experiencing an entirely new dimension of spiritual desire.

I began to pray because an unusual, quiet yearning had filled my heart. It grew as my heart was stirred and it became an intense longing, a thirst that felt impossible to quench. I used Song of Solomon 8:6 as a prayer. "Lord, seal me. Put fiery love in me. Seal me, Jesus." As words of desire began to pour from my lips, the desire for God felt stronger and stronger until it almost hurt. I began weeping, not from pain but from desire. The longing for Christ only became more intense. It was as if I was experiencing a divine vacuum that was actually drawing from God Himself. That drawing brought my heart into His presence in a new way.

As I felt the nearness of God, my desire for Him intensified. I could do little more than continue to weep, at first from passionate desire, and later from joy and gratitude for His nearness. I felt deeply grateful for who He is, for His love, His mercy, His truth and perfection, and I felt more grateful still to know with greater certainty than I'd ever imagined that He loved me so much and I really could love Him with all my heart and strength. Not wanting to lose the preciousness of the moment, I quietly buzzed my secretary and asked her not to let anyone or anything interrupt me for the next thirty minutes. I became totally immersed in the presence of God.

I had been worshiping at His feet for about fifteen minutes more when my secretary suddenly rang into my office. With irritation I asked her, "What are you doing? I don't want to be disturbed yet." "I'm sorry," she responded, "but you have a call, and he says it is very important that he speak to you right away." Annoyed at being distracted from these intimate moments with God, I picked up the phone. An acquaintance of mine was on the other end of the line. "Mike," he began excitedly, "I had a dream about you last night. The Lord has very clearly impressed upon me that I am to give you a particular verse as His message to you." My annoyance left as I listened to his words. "God wants you to set Him as a seal upon your heart."

God had answered me even as I entered into that secret time with Him. The vehement flames of His love are unquenchable and cannot be drowned. With this divine seal upon us, other things lose their dominance over our hearts.

WHOLEHEARTEDNESS IS ITS OWN REWARD

Some would consider wholeheartedness as our gift to the Lord, and in one sense it is. More than that, though, our passionate desire for God is *His* gift to *us*. In demanding our full attention, our full affection, and our full dedication to moving forward with Him, God sets the stage for a life of fullness.

When this longing to be wholehearted is answered by a life of radically pursuing God, then things deep within us align in ways we would have never dreamed possible. We are freed to become who we really are, without the limitations that half-hearted living creates. We begin to have larger capacities to love God and others, greater inclination to serve with happy hearts, and less difficulty obeying God's commands. God generously packages all this in such a way that we feel we're giving Him something; all the while He is smiling at us like a proud parent who knows He's really the one doing the giving. It is His desire, His jealous longing, that we love Him with all of our hearts, souls, minds, and strength, bringing us to this victorious place of intimate relationship with Him.

CHAPTER SEVEN

The Longing to Make a Deep and Lasting Impact

San Francisco artist David Best is known for building intricate monuments from delicately cut sheets of plywood. Often reaching fifty feet tall, they feature turrets, spindles and railings. These edifices are built in memory of people who have passed away. He leaves a stack of magic markers in the structures and encourages people to write messages about their deceased loved ones. The messages are a mix of profundity and pain. One message was a mix of both. Scrawled in green letters eight inches tall, it read: "Dad, what did your life mean?"

There was no story written alongside the question, so we can only imagine the circumstances driving someone to ask it. Whether the father in question was a good one or not is beside the point. The inference is this: "Dad, I watched you closely and cannot determine the impact you had. It would appear that even from a child's point of view, your life meant...*nothing*." Tragically, at the end of a parent's life, a child looked at his life story and could not perceive an obvious long-term impact on the world, for good or bad. Asked in a moment of private vulnerability, that simple question reveals a longing that exists in every human heart. It is an attempt to reconcile the temporal nature of this life with the eternal nature of the next one. Intuitively, people desire to make an impact. Most cannot bear the thought that the extent of their existence could be summed up in a few lines chiseled on a gravestone. There must be more.

Knowing we have limited time in this life, we all long to make a difference that will last far beyond our moment in time, confirming that our lives have meaning beyond the end of our days of flesh and blood. If the desire to have an impact is so much a part of the essence of what it means to have a human soul, surely that desire will not find its ultimate fulfillment in this age. It must come to fruition in the age to come. We are wired to make an impact for all eternity.

We were created to do that which is relevant and significant. God designed us to desperately want to make a difference in the lives of others. We need to know we are making a contribution that is significant to God and one He esteems and remembers forever. Being sure we are impacting people now, while at the same time achieving eternal reward in Heaven, satisfies this longing. A life of meaning involves living in a way that contributes to the enrichment of others in this life and in the age to come. Working together with Jesus to awaken other hearts in love is essential to our emotional health.

> I have no greater joy than to hear that my children
> walk in truth. (3 John 4)

The longing to make a relevant impact includes the longing for the heroic. By heroic, I mean being willing to risk losing everything so others can experience something significant and life-changing. We long to share things with others that change them or bring them joy and goodness; for example, when we receive great news about something and can't wait to tell the ones we love. When a five-year-old boy finds out his brother is getting a brand new bicycle for Christmas, he just has to tell the secret to see the brother explode with joy. We love being a part of that which exhilarates the people we love. When a woman wins the lottery, she will phone her family immediately to celebrate with them. When a terminal cancer patient receives some break-through medical cure, he can not contain himself from telling the other patients in the cancer ward. The desire to exhilarate others with good news is fundamental to our humanity.

FAITHFUL IN SMALL THINGS

> "And he said to him, 'Well done, good servant; be-cause you were faithful in a very little, have author-ity over ten cities.'" (Luke 19:17)

> "His lord said to him, 'Well done, good and faithful servant; you were faithful over a few things, I will make you ruler over many things. Enter into the joy of your lord.'" (Matthew 25:21)

God has called us to be faithful in small things, which tells us that small things are relevant because they are esteemed and remembered by God. He evaluates and rewards our lives in eter-nity based on the small things we have done in this age. Know-ing this gives us strength and quiet confidence to be faithful and diligent while instilling a sense of significance in us. This has a powerful effect on our hearts, motivating us to pursue lasting impact in this age and in the age to come.

We easily become preoccupied with seeking what looks and feels significant to us while devaluing faithfulness in the small things. However, eternal impact is mainly achieved through our faithfulness in small things. Only a few people in history have an international platform like Billy Graham or a worldwide eco-nomic reputation like a Bill Gates. When we think about it we realize that God has called only a few to do large things. Of the billions of people in history, *all of them* are called to be faithful in small things. To some this is synonymous with insignificance or irrelevance. Nothing could be further from the truth. God promises that if we are faithful in the everyday scenarios with little public acknowledgment, He will esteem and remember them forever. We can make a lasting impact in God's kingdom by being faithful in small things.

> *Until I was nineteen years old, my idea of impact was limited to how many thousands of lives I could touch in this life. I distinctly remember the day my paradigm changed. Since then, the Lord has been continually reworking my idea of what impact looks like in this world.*
>
> *One evening after a prayer meeting, Mike Bickle asked me a question. "Where do you see yourself in ten years?" Believing I had the right answer, I told him of my plans to have a big, impacting ministry that would bring many people to the Lord. Mike responded with a surprising question. "How many people were with Jesus at the end of His earthly ministry just before He died?" He only had a few faithful disciples after almost four years of ministry, yet the Father considered Him successful.*
>
> *What became clear to me is how differently God views our impact in this life. The Leader of the hosts of heaven did not gather a large group of loyal followers on earth. At the time of His crucifixion, even His closest friends declined to be associated with Him. Yet this same Man, scorned by the majority during His earthly ministry, will reign throughout the ages as the King of the kings and Lord of lords.*
>
> *Though God designed us with a desire to make a deep and lasting impact and to live in a significant way, we must understand how God views this. Lasting impact will not come through pride and self-promotion. Rather, it is the result of a meek life. Jesus taught us that many who are first in honor and privilege will be last, and the last will be first (Matthew 19:30). While few embrace this truth right now, the day will come when we will all understand just how true it is. —Deborah Hiebert*

WHY ARE WE HERE?

We play a small but significant role in a very large drama, in a great conflict with eternal consequences. We are not some footnote to the script. God did not create the world because He was bored. He is not peering down on us as if we were a collection of highly-functional gerbils in a cage, wondering what we're going to do next. He is looking for people who will partner with Him to bring about His purposes on Earth, and ultimately function as the Bride of Jesus, equally-yoked and madly in love with His Son.

Viewed through the bridal paradigm, our contribution is much more significant than most people dare to dream. We will rule and reign alongside His Son forever. He calls us co-heirs for a reason. He wants us to have eternal impact and an eternal role in the story He is unfolding. Jesus gave instructions along this line in the final moments before He ascended to be with the Father. He made it clear that God's plan for earth includes the willing cooperation of His people. He charged us to make a lasting impact on the nations. "Go therefore and make disciples of all the nations…" (Matthew 28:19).

God has big plans for people, real people like you and me. Speaking to His little band of followers, who were mostly un-educated and remarkably unremarkable, He laid out their future: *You will disciple nations.* Jesus launched a global mission that would impact their lives, even into eternity. God is looking for people who want to make a deep and lasting impact, people who will partner with Him on a level far exceeding just working a job or pursuing personal happiness.

While some might think of the desire for lasting impact as innately self-serving, it is not. Neither is it a sign of weakness or vanity. It's an expression of being created in the likeness of God. Historically, some people in the Church have dismissed this desire, confusing it with ungodly ambition or pride. They claim that to dedicate energy to making an impact now is to strive for self-importance or fleeting prestige. The fact is that we are very important, but only have lasting significance as we walk in obedience to God's will for our lives. The longing to make a deep and lasting impact is partially satisfied as we engage in changing the lives of others, which in turn results in eternal rewards of our own.

MAKING A DIFFERENCE IN THE LIVES OF OTHERS

Our God-given desires include our longing to contribute to the lives of others, those we care about as well as those we've never met. The most common expression of this is our desire to impact the lives of our children in a long-term and permanent way. We want to influence not only their immediate decisions, but also their decision-making process. We hope that even when we are gone, our children will reflect on what they've learned from us and respond accordingly. We see it in familiar phrases. "Your mother taught you well..." "You sure make your parents proud..." "The apple doesn't fall far from the tree..." "You're a chip off the old block..." "I can see you were raised well."

We also have a drive to make a difference with friends and coworkers. As we get to know them better, the Lord begins to reveal to us His heart for them. The fellow sitting at the next desk becomes a child of God in our eyes. The neighbor across the street grows dear to us and we think, "What can I do to bless her life?" Once we taste God's love, we become zealous to impart it to others. We are not content to explore the vastness of God's love alone. As we grow in the Lord, we feel compelled to impact more people than just those close to us. We begin to pray for the waitress who serves us, we begin to prophesy to the stranger in the grocery store. We find ourselves unwilling to go through life self-contained—we must make an impact.

All of this is part of the grand plan of God to impart His heart to us. He gives us these desires with the expressed intent of partnering with us. Given the choice of doing it with us or without us, He makes it clear that His perfect plan includes our imperfect cooperation. He doesn't *need* our participation, He *wants* it.

SHARING WHAT HAS IMPACTED US

We love to talk to others about what blesses us. One phenomenon of the last decade was the resurgence of Apple computers after the initial runaway success enjoyed by Microsoft. Apple owes its survival and resurgence to a small but vocal group of users who would tell anyone who would listen, "This Apple computer is so much better than that computer...it's ultra-simple to use, it's intuitive, and it helps me be more productive. I love it, I wouldn't trade it for the world, and I'll never use another Windows machine again." This led to the coining of the phrase, "Mac Evangelists," computer users with such an evangelistic fervor for the Apple Macintosh that you might assume they're getting a free toaster for converting a PC user to Apple. Not so: they are simply demonstrating the human trait that eagerly shares what blesses them.

Any time something has had a big impact on us, we are driven to share it. The dad who read the book that helped him in his relationship with his son immediately buys a copy to give to his friends so they can have the same experience. The mom who suddenly gains insight that helps her with her toddler's behavior wants to tell other moms what worked for her. The scientist who, after years of scribbling on napkins, finally completes a groundbreaking equation will do all he can to publicize his discovery. He will deliver lectures to any group of people who will listen. Essentially, we are driven to share with others that which brings us joy. This ability to bring joy and make an impact on others is something put in our hearts by the God who loves people. Without this sense of impact on others, we lose something dynamic.

Our sense of relevance is often connected with doing something that exhilarates others. We delight to share things that cause others to be exhilarated. There is something glorious about telling good news to those we love. Stories touch people's hearts, and when we have one to tell, we usually can't wait to share it. Think of Bartimaeus, the blind beggar from the city of Jericho who was healed by Jesus (Mark 10:46; Luke 18:35). Imagine the joy Bartimaeus had in telling his blind friends about his encounter with Jesus. How exhilarating to bring that news to them! Imagine how he felt when he told them Jesus was in the area. We love to communicate news that excites our friends. We are exhilarated in their exhilaration, and joyful when good things happen that bring joy to others.

> For unclean spirits...came out of many...and many who were paralyzed and lame were healed. There was great joy in that city. (Acts 8:7-8)

There is something that makes us want to shout good news from the rooftops in hopes that others can be saved some of the heartaches we've encountered. The idea of changing the trajectory of another person's life is irresistible. We're unsatisfied with wasting small talk on golf clubs or garden tools or the weather. We want to impart substance to people. We want to say and do things that mean something. It's a part of our desire to make a deep and lasting impact.

WE FULFILL THE CALL OF GOD THROUGH INFLUENCE

Influence is a strange thing to understand. Most people grossly underestimate how much influence they have. They are convinced that no one ever listens to or watches them and that nobody will ever remember what they've said or done. Influence is difficult to quantify, but the weight of it is felt in tangible ways. If influence is measured by volume, then the most influential person on the planet is a rock star. If influence is measured by fervency, it's highly likely that the most influential person on the planet is a young Muslim with a bomb in his backpack.

In truth, these two people may entertain or frighten millions, but neither truly influences many in the long run. They make a splash in the pond of time, but neither creates a current that moves people or things in a lasting way. A person who is truly influential possesses the ability to affect the long-term decisions and quality of life of others. They have the capacity to produce lasting change in the hearts and behavior of people. Only God has all the information necessary to evaluate true influence and impact.

While we rightfully associate influence with power, there is an ironic twist to how it works in the kingdom of God. From God's perspective, influence is usually released with a whisper. It is the kind word spoken to the harried co-worker. It is the glance of approval or the word of appreciation given to an eager child or a friend. Its power lies not in volume or shock value, but in consistency and sincerity. Ask someone who has made the deepest, most lasting impact on them and they will usually tell you about someone they have observed over an extended period of time. While we may be temporarily wowed by stage presence and pizzazz, deep within we are impacted most by the people who walk out their commitments with daily consistency. This approach to life is the one valued by God. It is called faithfulness, and it operates in meekness. God sees, esteems, remembers, and then rewards the labors of love done for others out of love for Him, and promises to always remember every word or deed in service to others for the sake of His name.

> For God is not unjust to forget your work and labor of love which you have shown toward His name, in that you have ministered to the saints. (Hebrews 6:10)

> "Whoever gives one of these little ones only a cup of cold water in the name of a disciple, assuredly, I say to you, he shall by no means lose his reward." (Matthew 10:42)

Jesus taught that using our money to do acts of kindness in this age will be remembered and have an impact on our relationships in the age to come. In fact, Jesus said that when we give money to people in this life and meet them in the age to come, they will remember our sacrificial gifts.

> "I say to you, make friends for yourselves by unrighteous mammon, that when you fail, they may receive you into an everlasting home." (Luke 16:9)

THE NATURE OF DEEP AND LASTING IMPACT

Billy Graham is clearly one of the most influential Christians in the last one hundred years. He has conducted huge stadium crusades around the world. Untold millions have heard his simple presentation of the gospel and many have responded by coming to Christ. In recent years, his health has restricted his public appearances considerably and his sermons have been considerably shortened. But the content has not changed one iota. Anyone going to a Billy Graham crusade can bank on one thing—a straightforward presentation of the gospel of Jesus, followed by an opportunity to repent of sin and accept Him as Lord and Savior.

I went to his evangelistic crusade at Arrowhead Stadium in Kansas City, held in June of 2005. As when I first heard him in person at the Cotton Bowl Stadium in 1972, he was faithful to His message. I have followed Billy Graham for more than thirty years with great admiration and respect. He has been a picture of consistency in his presentation of the truth of Jesus. After decades of high-profile ministry, there are two questions in peoples' minds when he takes to the podium. "Is this the last crusade?" and "Who will follow in his footsteps?"

The question "Who will be the next Billy Graham?" says volumes about how we view influence. We may not verbalize it, but some think that the main way multitudes will be saved is through stadium-style events. However, very little evangelism actually happens in large stadium events. That's not to say that it is not a genuine ministry; it's a wonderful example of God partnering with a person to bring forth His purposes, but it's not the norm. In all likelihood, more people get saved at neighborhood barbecues and in the lunchroom at work than in the one big stadium event—and certainly more get discipled through simpler, smaller everyday encounters. Christianity was not designed to be a particularly high-profile affair orchestrated by a tiny conclave of leaders. There may never be another Billy Graham, but neither will there be another you, and both you and Billy have a calling from God to be a person of influence.

In setting the wheels in motion for His millennial kingdom, Jesus knew He must set some sort of standard by which our impact would be measured and our greatness rewarded. What He taught is profound in its balance of simplicity and difficulty: serving with meekness. This is something everyone can do. Jesus' kingdom operates and increases in this way. His kingdom will be advanced by those with a radical commitment to serving. Yes, the first commandment is to love Him with all of our hearts, but the second commandment is to love our neighbors with the same forgiving, selfless love with which we love ourselves. Serving is the measuring stick for making a lasting impact! We don't have to choose between making an impact in this life or impacting our quality of life in the next. We can do both, and, in fact, we are instructed to.

IMPACT IN THIS AGE

In the early 1980s, a certain gentleman planted a church in Cincinnati. In the early years, he drove a school bus by day while meeting with people in the evenings to share his vision for a church. He realized early on that he was no Billy Graham. He also knew Billy Graham wasn't called to specifically reach Cincinnati; he was. One day, while sitting in line at a Taco Bell drive-thru, this gentleman felt the Lord speak to him. "If you take the people no one wants, I will give you thousands of them."

With around fifty people in his struggling church, he felt God challenge him to serve the poor of Cincinnati and thus influence people by kindness. It wasn't preaching in a stadium he was being asked to do, but continued faithfulness in simple and small acts of service to others. Out of a heartfelt desire to make a lasting impact on the city of Cincinnati, he sought for practical ways to express the love of God. Twenty years later, his church is home to six thousand people. On the front of the church building, in large lettering, is this inscription:

Small things done with great love will change the world.

IMPACT IN THE AGE TO COME

The goal of impacting lives is excellent, but incomplete. While many people find legitimate fulfillment in serving others, we want our lives to count in eternity as well. Fortunately, that is where we have the greatest potential for impact: not impact on another person for a few decades, or even on our culture for a century, but impact on the entire world as well as our own lives for eternity. Many Christians divorce their actions in this life from their impact in the next. The second coming of Christ has been portrayed as some sort of cosmic delete button, after which nothing that happened in this life will matter, or even be remembered. Well-meaning Christians have drawn a line of distinction between this temporal life and the fullness in which we will walk on earth during the age to come.

Scripture, however, makes it clear that there is a lot of continuity between the two time frames. Therefore, what we do as Christians now will matter then. If there were no continuity between the two realities, we would be squandering our lives. This is not the case. Instead, we are building relationships, honing skills, and shaping our character in practical ways that will make a significant difference in eternity. As we fashion our lives in this age, we must keep in mind the greatness of the age to come and that the small things done in obedience and meekness now will result in greatness and impact then. There is a divine exchange coming to our lives. Many will find that the kingdoms they built in this life will be taken from them, while those who have maintained meek hearts throughout their earthly lives will receive great authority and honor. When we really understand this exchange rate, we will invest all we can in what God values.

> Peter answered and said to Him, "See, we have left all and followed You. Therefore what shall we have?" So Jesus said to them, "Assuredly I say to you, that in the regeneration, when the Son of Man sits on the throne of His glory, you who have followed Me

> will also sit on twelve thrones, judging the twelve
> tribes of Israel. And everyone who has left houses
> or brothers or sisters or father or mother or wife or
> children or lands, for My name's sake, shall receive a
> hundredfold, and inherit eternal life. But many who
> are first will be last, and the last first." (Matthew
> 19:27-30)

Believers in Jesus are those who have a great opportunity to pursue a deep and lasting impact in this age and in the age to come. In the Sermon on the Mount (Matthew 5-7), we are taught to give to our enemies, to fast, to pray, and to bless others. Those attitudes are often rejected by this age, but they will impact our eternal destinies. When the Lord returns, He will establish righteousness worldwide (Isaiah 2:1-4; 9:6-7; 11:1-16). However, before He comes, there will be worldwide revival that will cause new pockets of righteousness and justice to be established in many parts of society. The Lord will protect and sustain some of the justice that is established in society in the end-time revival. We labor today, knowing that some of our labors in establishing justice in the earth will withstand the pressures of the evil one, even those coming from the Antichrist and his approaching reign of terror.

There will be some continuity of our labors; the fasting, the prayer, and the acts of mercy will not just disappear when He returns. The prayers we have prayed for our home town will not suddenly become void and invalid after the Lord returns. In fact, they will become an even more certain reality! Some of the ground we gain in righteousness and justice in society will serve as a part of the beachhead from which Jesus will rule in our cities when He returns to earth. Some people get the idea that studying the end times leads people to disconnect from the tasks at hand—nothing could be further from the truth. Our fervent belief in the Lord's return must not cause us to abdicate our responsibility to work toward change in society. Just the opposite is true—*because* He is coming, we work to change society. We work for justice because we understand the implications of His imminent arrival. He will continue to increase that which He established through His Church before His coming.

We must consider the ultimate meaning of the work to which we are putting our hands. If we're leading a small band of intercessors, the intercession we are making is preparing the ground for a kingdom that will last a thousand years. Some of the children we are training on Sunday mornings may be mighty men and women of God who will do great exploits outlasting their natural earthly lives. The humility that we work hard to develop in this life will contribute to determining our roles in the millennial kingdom and the eternal age.

LIVING WITH A DESIRE FOR IMPACT

For too long, the enemy has used our desire to make a lasting impact as ammunition against us. "You just want to be seen," he accuses. "All you want is to build your own reputation. You want a plaque with your name on it on a wall somewhere." Like most falsehoods, these statements sting, because there is a small measure of truth to them. All of us struggle with this in varying degrees. We have all lived with conflicting feelings over this desire since we were old enough to verbalize it. In fact, we learned quickly not to verbalize it because it would usually be misunderstood and criticized. We have learned to keep such thoughts and longings to ourselves. Some of us eventually trained ourselves to not even think that way.

Fortunately, the Lord knows that for which we were created. He dictated the story that demands people to do great things and then planted those desires deep within us. The Holy Spirit witnesses within us as we long to be people who do things significant in God's sight. Great things are attainable by those who love God with their whole hearts.

CONCLUSION

September 8, 1941 was a day that charted the life course of nearly three million people. It was the day that Hitler's forces laid siege to Leningrad as part of his campaign against Russia. Surrounded by German troops and under constant bombardment, the residents of the historic city hunkered down for the duration. Many wondered how long the city could survive the onslaught of the enemy. Would this continue for days, weeks, months? On that autumn day, many might have feared, but few could have known they would be under the heavy hand of the Nazis for nearly two and a half years.

Within the city, fuel and food reserves were only sufficient to last two months at the most. Life grew hard almost immediately. Public transportation ceased, food was rationed. By the first winter, there was no heat, no water, and very little food. A few hundred thousand people were evacuated via a road built across a frozen lakebed, but more than 640,000 would die. Until the siege was fully lifted in January 1944, the city was a picture of tortuous waiting: millions of people waiting for a deliverer to come in the form of a Soviet counter-offensive.

When I read about the siege of Leningrad, it reminded me of the way many people view their Christian walks. Lives that should be marked with joy and freedom are instead fraught with difficulty and pain. People have the mentality of being under an enemy siege. We vow never to surrender to Satan, yet we suffer with our basic desires remaining unfulfilled. As Leningrad lacked food and electricity, our souls lack fulfillment and we see the enemy as one who can keep us from satisfaction. With this mindset, we become like souls under siege.

If you receive anything from this book, let it be this: life in Christ was never intended to be lived as a besieged soul. It is not a life of just getting by and trying to hang on until the end. While we do look forward to the return of Christ, we also live with the truth that He is alive and His Spirit is within us now. There is a river of superior pleasure designed to be a fountain of life in our inner man if we say yes to it and drink from it vigorously.

God delights in fascinating and exhilarating our hearts. We don't have to live bored lives. Each day is to be filled with new discoveries. We are not under siege. We can be victorious. Our victory is made tangible as God answers the longings of our hearts now in time and space. He has written the love story of the ages and chosen the perfect context in which longing and fulfillment unite in a beautiful dance. Greatness, intimacy without shame, the potential for long-term impact, and the other longings of our hearts, do not lie outside the cities of our hearts, cordoned off by the forces of evil. Certainly, there is a real enemy and there is a real war going on, but our Commander is well able to keep us supplied and our souls fulfilled.

Not only does God have plans for us to overcome the enemy, He desires to exhilarate us in love in the presence of the enemy (Psalm 23:5). Most people turn to God as a last resort. They do all they can to fulfill the longings of their hearts with entertainment, possessions, or relationships with other broken people, only to find that these create an even greater void. In time, the scaffolding they have built to keep their souls propped up falls apart. Yet God appears in their emptiness. At first their cold hearts cannot even respond, but as the fire of His love softens and warms them, a miracle takes place. Life appears. A heartbeat is heard. It is perhaps faint at first, but growing in strength and purpose. Over time, they find themselves standing before Him, more fascinated with pure love and truth than they ever were with false fulfillment.

For more than seven years, I have had the privilege of leading the International House of Prayer with Deborah and others on my leadership team. Even as I write this, the prayer and worship continue. Our weak prayers ascend to the Father and mingle with the prayers of all the saints from all over the world and throughout church history. Every two hours another worship team steps in to replace the team just before. We were warned that young people simply would not do this, that they would not commit to prayer, and that if they did commit, they wouldn't keep those commitments. Nevertheless, seven years in, it is the young people who are leading in the prayer room. It is not uncommon for the average age in the room to be around twenty.

It is an incredible blessing to labor alongside young people, old people, single and married people, children, and everyone in between, all of whom have upended their personal lives to be a part of a perpetual solemn assembly. They raise their own financial support as intercessory missionaries. Several hundred are students at International House of Prayer University, our full-time Bible school, where we endeavor to redefine theological education in the context of night-and-day prayer. Hundreds more set aside three or six months of their lives to participate in an internship. They come from every state in the country, a number of nations around the world, and every station in life. They have something in common: they are on the pathway to being fulfilled in and by God.

To say they are set on this path is not to say they don't have times of emptiness and unmet emotional needs. They struggle with relationships and needs like everyone else, but they have found something most people never find. Having rejected the materialistic and entertainment-driven culture surrounding them, they have found that the longings of their hearts are only truly fulfilled in knowing and pursuing God. Fortunately, this fulfillment is by no means reserved for our staff or those who end up moving to Kansas City to be in our 24/7 prayer room. It has been found by millions of others around the world and throughout history.

You may have come to this understanding early in your walk with the Lord, or stumbled into it after a lifetime of pain. However you arrive at this conclusion, you will find what you are looking for when you realize that God has placed those longings in your heart as a divine desire; your hunger is a gift from God to draw you to Him. It's a holy want with a holy fulfillment. Everything you really need and want is offered by and found in Him.

Have you pursued the fulfillment of the longings of your heart by chasing after cheap imitations? Has your craving for greatness led to years of self-centered behavior? Has your drive to find intimacy bound you in a pattern of shame? Have you sold your soul at too cheap a price—and too often? The fact that you want your longings fulfilled points to the truth of what I am saying: no one hungers and longs for what does not exist. The good news is that your past failures can really be things of the past, your present can be radically changed, and your future can be glorious as you seek to find your fulfillment in Jesus, the beautiful God. It is found by continually placing your heart before Him and asking Him to reveal His heart to you. In this, your longings will be progressively fulfilled.

You may have kept yourself from the obvious sinful behaviors that the multitudes fall into, yet on the inside you are just as dead and unfulfilled. During the Siege of Leningrad, just as many people suffered from boredom as hunger. This boredom led to depression as they saw the months go by with no indication that freedom was really coming, that it was, in fact, within their grasp. For those who linger around the fringe of what God wants, I urge you to step in and determinedly seek the fullness. Drawing near to the Father will stir up these desires even as He fulfills them. God's great plan is for your desire to lead you to Him. Everything He placed within you is meant to bring you into the fullest, most intimate, most joyful relationship with Him. While it may bring frustration and ache at times, it is a holy frustration, a sacred ache, and God will meet you there. After all, God's image is stamped on your soul.

Your longings, if you let them, will be what draw you into the Divine. Like separate streams, each of these seven longings is an escort into the eternal ocean of God's fiery affections. There is nothing more beautiful than when all your longings unite as one holy, raging river of yearning that drives you to God.

I remember when I began to experience this a little more in my own life. I wasn't primarily looking to friends, food, or entertainment to answer the burning cries in my heart; I was looking to God. Though the ache was often painful, I remember thinking, "This is what I was made for. I was made for love. I was made for God." Aching and longing is beautiful. It is a gift because this ache is for God alone. I knew God was smiling at me and that it was only a matter of time before He would answer. I felt like I was really living as I was created to live. Even in the delay, before my longings were fulfilled, my spirit was positioned, my heart was alive, and eternity was weighing down on me.

Recently, one of the young ladies at the International House of Prayer encouraged a leader with these wise words, "Your desire will be your compass until Jesus comes." With that thought in mind, grab your Bible, quiet your heart, mind your compass, and begin your journey with the eternal longings of your heart. You were made to long. You were made for God. He *will* answer.

INTERNATIONAL HOUSE *of* PRAYER

....

24/7 LIVE WORSHIP AND PRAYER

ihopkc.org/prayerroom

....

Since September 19, 1999, we have continued in night-and-day prayer with worship as the foundation of our ministry to win the lost, heal the sick, and make disciples, as we labor alongside the larger Body of Christ to see the Great Commission fulfilled, and to function as forerunners who prepare the way for the return of Jesus.

By the grace of God, we are committed to combining 24/7 prayers for justice with 24/7 works of justice until the Lord returns. We believe we are better equipped to reach out to others when our lives are rooted in prayer that focuses on intimacy with God and intercession for breakthrough of the fullness of God's power and purpose for this generation.

The Best *of the* Prayer Room Live

SIX LIVE WORSHIP ALBUMS PER YEAR

....

Every other month we release a new volume of worship
and prayer recordings from our Global Prayer Room.

Subscribe today at **ihopkc.org/bestof**

International House of Prayer Missions Base, 3535 E. Red Bridge Road, Kansas City, MO 64137
(816) 763-0200 | info@ihopkc.org

INTERNATIONAL
HOUSE *of* PRAYER
U N I V E R S I T Y

MINISTRY · MUSIC · MEDIA · MISSIONS

··

ENCOUNTER GOD. DO HIS WORKS. CHANGE THE WORLD.
ihopkc.org/ihopu

··

International House of Prayer University (IHOPU) is a full-time Bible school which exists to equip this generation in the Word and in the power of the Holy Spirit for the bold proclamation of the Lord Jesus and His return.

As part of the International House of Prayer, our Bible school is built around the centrality of the Word and 24/7 prayer with worship, equipping students in the Word and the power of the Spirit for the bold proclamation of the Lord Jesus and His kingdom. Training at IHOPU forms not only minds but also lifestyle and character, to sustain students for a life of obedience, humility, and anointed service in the kingdom. Our curriculum combines in-depth biblical training with discipleship, practical service, outreach, and works of compassion.

IHOPU is for students who long to encounter Jesus. With schools of ministry, music, media, and missions, our one- to four-year certificate and diploma programs prepare students to engage in the Great Commission and obey Jesus' commandments to love God and people.

> "What Bible School has 'prayer' on its curriculum? The most important thing a man can study is the prayer part of the Book. But where is this taught?
>
> Let us strip off the last bandage and declare that many of our presidents and teachers do not pray, shed no tears, know no travail. Can they teach what they do not know?"
>
> –Leonard Ravenhill, *Why Revival Tarries*

International House of Prayer University, 12901 S. US Highway 71, Grandview, MO 64030
(816) 763-0243 | info@ihopu.org

International House *of* Prayer
INTERNSHIPS

INTRO TO IHOPKC • FIRE IN THE NIGHT • ONE THING INTERNSHIP
SIMEON COMPANY • HOPE CITY INTERNSHIP

ihopkc.org/internships

Internships exist to see people equipped with the Word of God, ministering in the power of the Holy Spirit, engaged in intercession, and committed to outreach and service.

Our five internships are three to six months long and accommodate all seasons of life. The purpose of the internships is to further prepare individuals of all ages as intercessors, worshipers, messengers, singers, and musicians for the work of the kingdom. While each internship has a distinctive age limit, length, and schedule, they all share the same central training components: corporate prayer and worship meetings, classroom instruction, practical ministry experience, outreach, and relationship-building.

Biblical teaching in all of the internships focuses on intimacy with Jesus, ministry in the power of the Holy Spirit, the forerunner ministry, evangelizing the lost, justice, and outreach. Interns also receive practical, hands-on training in the prophetic and healing ministries.

Upon successful completion of a six-month internship or two three-month tracks, some will stay and apply to join IHOPKC staff.

Our IHOPKC Leadership Team

Our leadership team of over a hundred and fifty men and women, with diversity of experience, background, and training, represent twenty countries and thirty denominations and oversee eighty-five departments on our missions base. With a breadth of experience in pastoral ministry, missions work, education, and the marketplace, this team's training in various disciplines includes over forty master's degrees and ten doctorates.

International House of Prayer Missions Base, 3535 E. Red Bridge Road, Kansas City, MO 64137
(816) 763-0200 | internships@ihopkc.org

MIKE BICKLE
TEACHING LIBRARY
—— *Free Teaching & Resource Library* ——

This International House of Prayer resource library, encompassing more than thirty years of Mike's teaching ministry, provides access to hundreds of resources in various formats, including streaming video, downloadable video, and audio, accompanied by study notes and transcripts, absolutely free of charge.

You will find some of Mike's most requested titles, including *The Gospel of Grace*; *The First Commandment*; *Jesus, Our Magnificent Obsession*; *Romans: Theology of Holy Passion*; *The Sermon on the Mount: The Kingdom Lifestyle*; and much more.

We encourage you to freely copy any of these teachings to share with others or use in any way: "our copyright is the right to copy." Older messages are being prepared and uploaded from Mike's teaching archives, and all new teachings are added immediately.

Visit mikebickle.org

International House of Prayer Missions Base, 3535 E. Red Bridge Road, Kansas City, MO 64137
(816) 763-0200 | info@ihopkc.org | ihopkc.org